PEANUTS®

Lunch Bag Cookbook

PEANUTS®
Lunch Bag Cookbook

PACKABLE SNACKS, SANDWICHES & TASTY TREATS

weldon**owen**

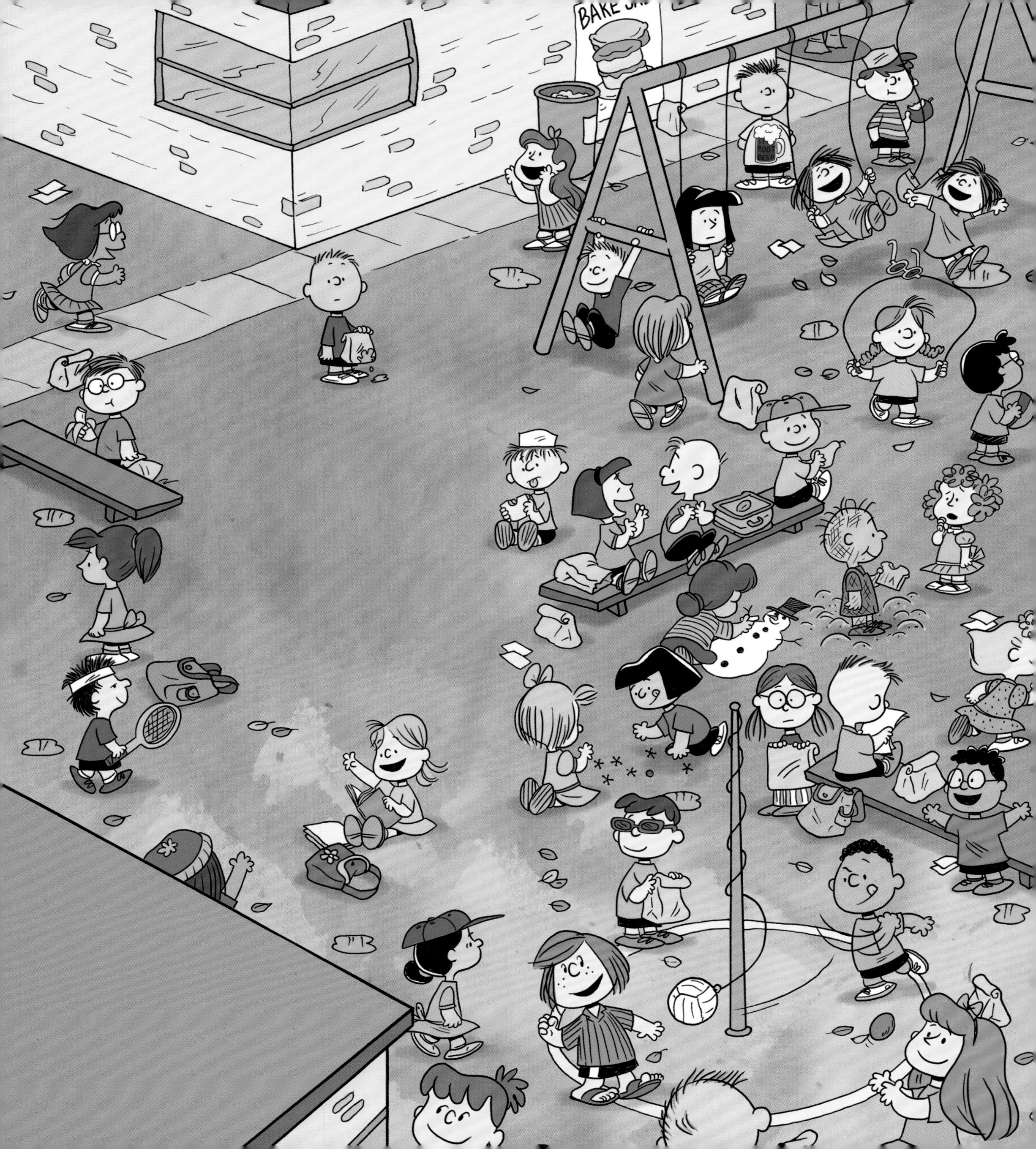

BAKE
ROOT BEER

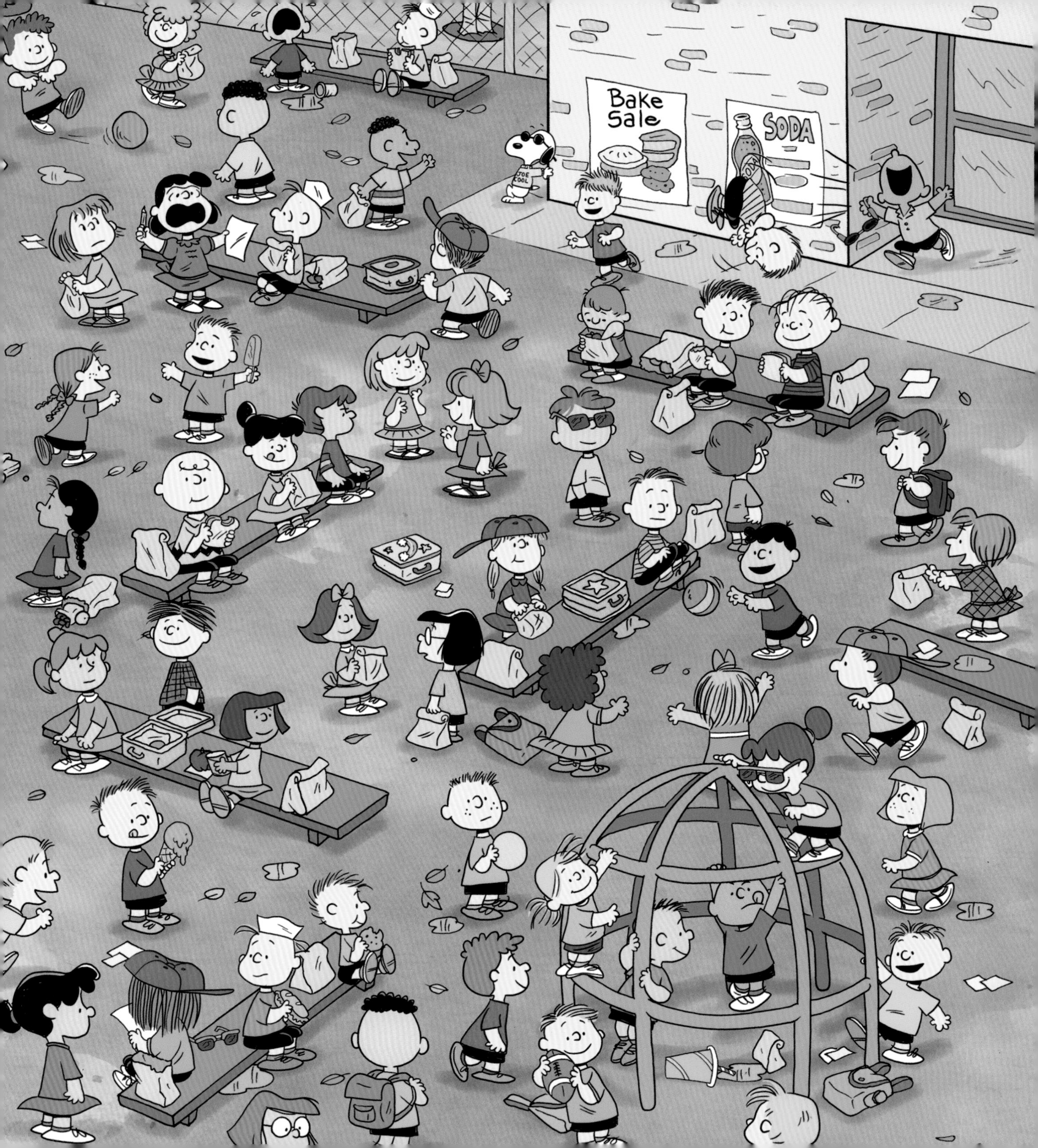

JOE COOL
Bake Sale
SODA

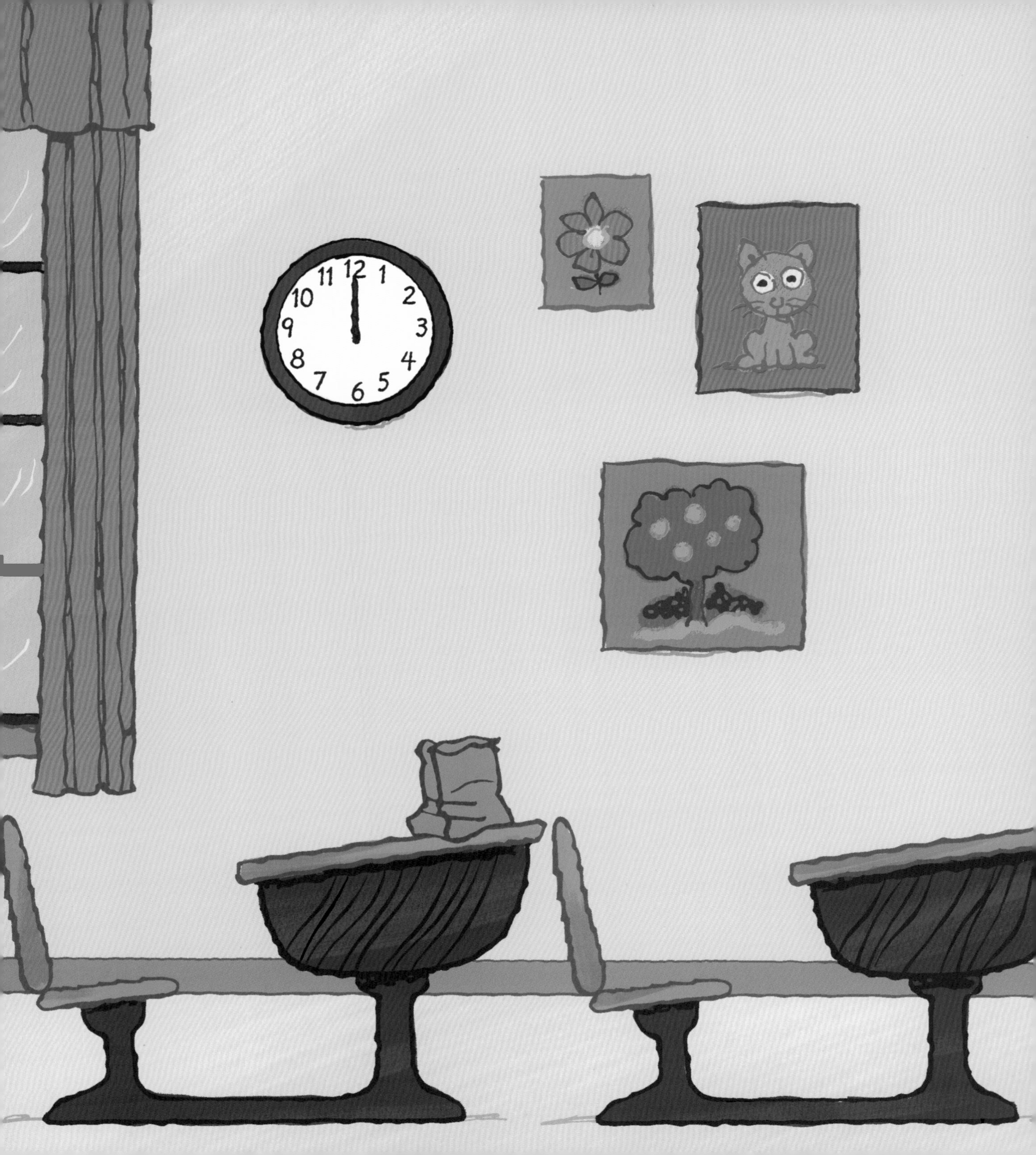

CONTENTS

INTRODUCTION

Kid-friendly, nutritious, and delicious—

all you need for a lunch bag! From healthy sandwiches and hearty soups to fun snacks and delectable sweets, the *Peanuts* gang serves up yummy ideas for all your kids' midday meals. They will delight in munching on snacks on a stick, finding new flavors in lunchtime classics, or dipping French toast "fingers" in blueberry-maple syrup.

Many of the recipes are perfect for big family-style meals from which leftovers can be used to make lunches. Many are fun for kids to help prepare. Many are special treats for those extra-special occasions and all are meant to inspire—just as Charles M. Schulz's beloved characters do.

Schulz valued family mealtime, and that joy, humor, wisdom—and occasional angst—is shared with you here. Join the *Peanuts* gang and mix and match lunch-time treats to provide year-round fun and yum!

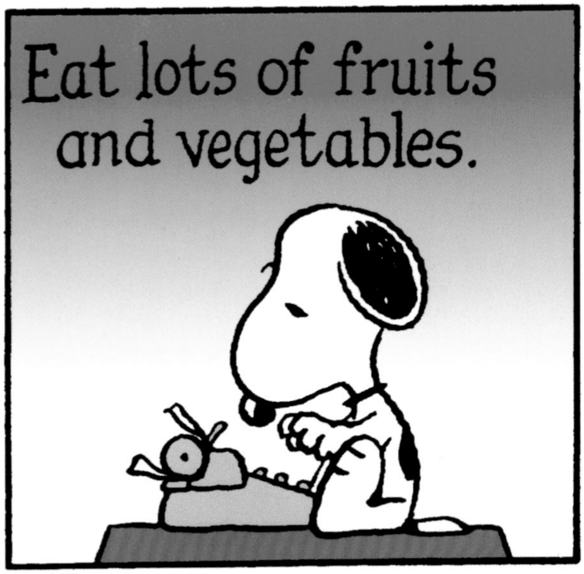
Eat lots of fruits and vegetables.

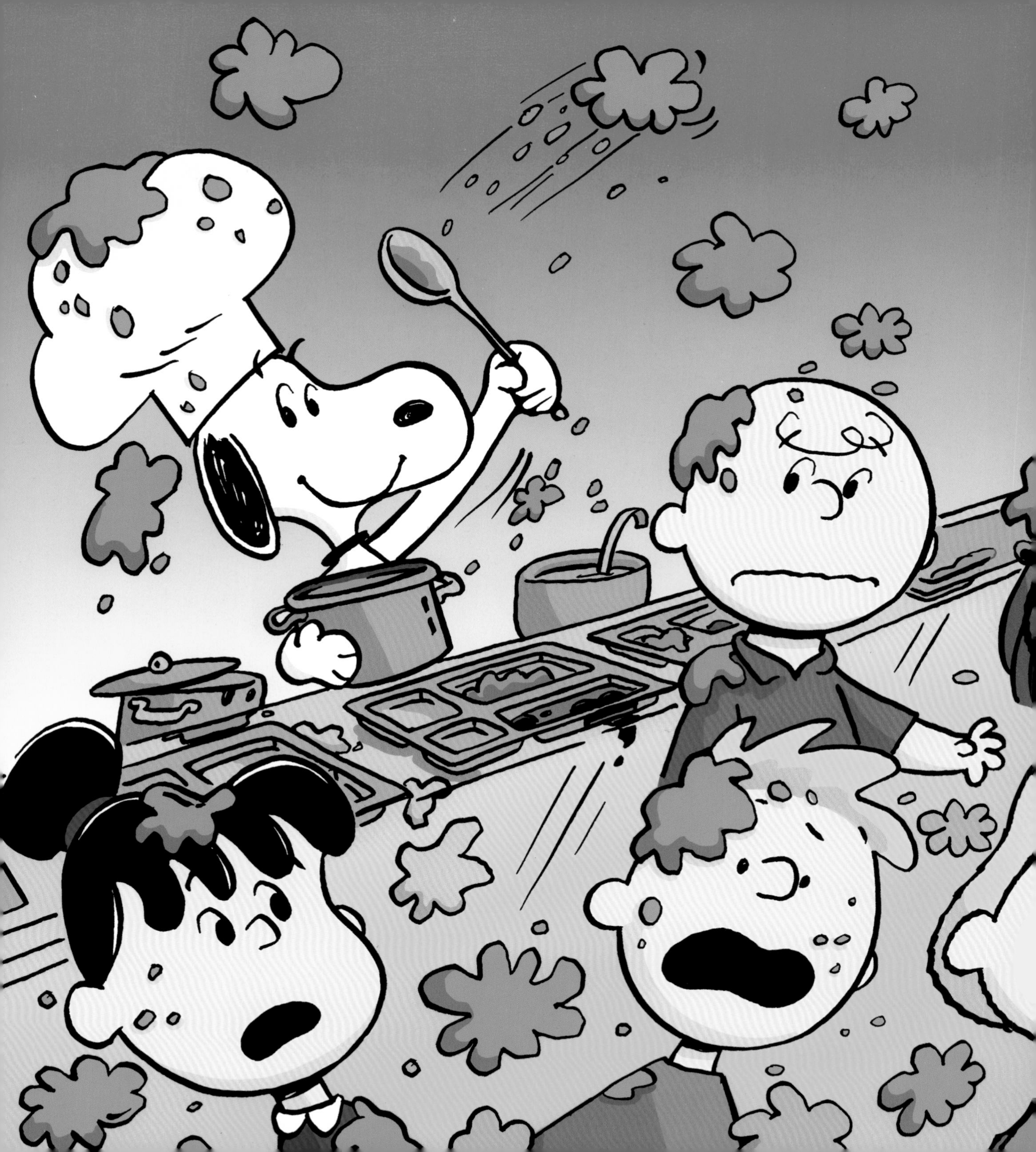

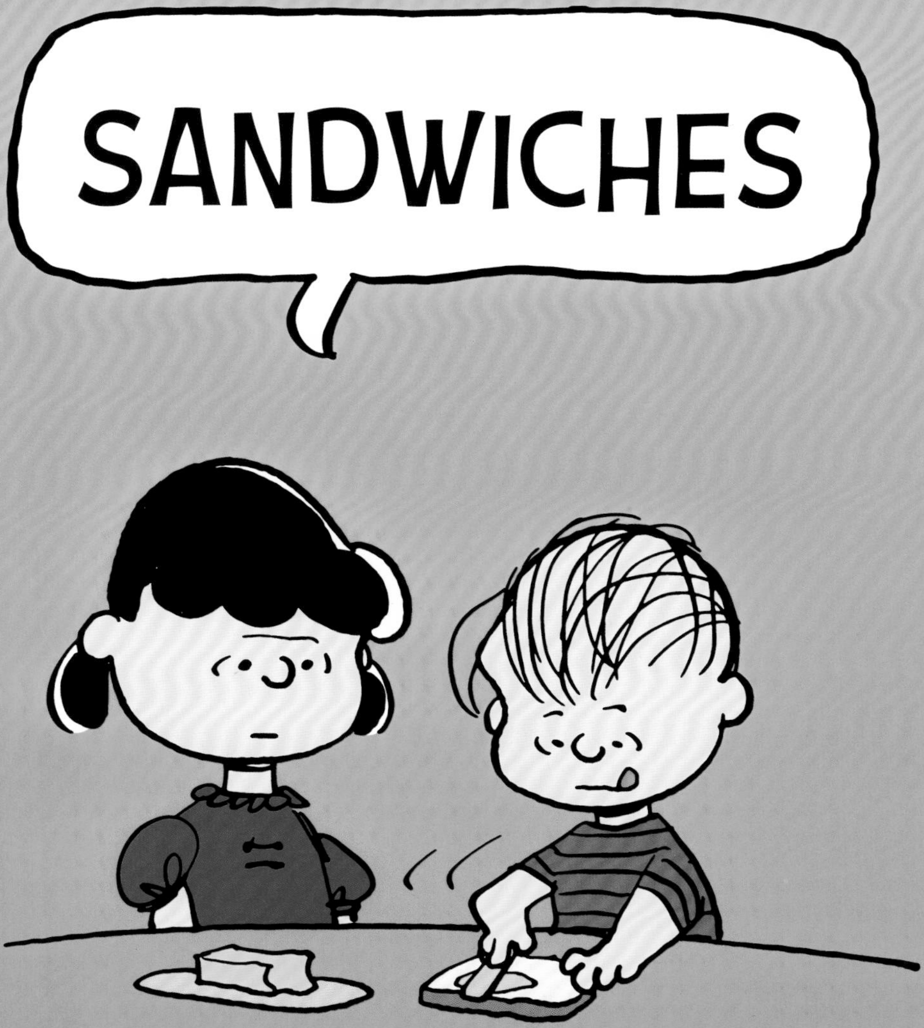
SANDWICHES

PEANUTS
I ALWAYS LIKE TO STOP ON MY WAY TO SCHOOL, AND CHECK TO SEE WHAT MOM PUT IN MY LUNCH...
A CHEESE SANDWICH, A BAG OF POTATO CHIPS, AN ORANGE, A CUP CAKE AND A NOTE...
2-16
"STUDY HARD, AND SOMEDAY YOU MAY GET TO BE PRESIDENT"
I'M THE ONLY PERSON I KNOW WHO GETS A LUNCH WITH A COMMERCIAL IN IT!
SCHULZ

LINUS'S NOTEWORTHY TURKEY WRAP

What could be better than a handwritten note of encouragement placed in your lunch box? An enticing turkey wrap rolled with love.

INGREDIENTS

1 whole-wheat tortilla
1 tablespoon honey mustard
¼ lb thinly sliced roasted turkey
¼ lb Brie cheese, cut lengthwise into 4 equal slices
¼ Granny Smith apple, cored and thinly sliced into half-moons
2 leaves butter lettuce

Makes 1 wrap

1 Slather 1 side of the wrap with the honey mustard. Place the turkey slices in the center of the wrap. Top the portion of turkey with 4 slices of cheese. Arrange the apple slices and then the butter lettuce on top of the cheese. Gently fold over the sides of the wrap and fold up snugly like a burrito.

2 Cut the wrap in half on the diagonal. Wrap each half in aluminum foil or arrange in an airtight container and close tightly. Refrigerate until ready to go, then pack in an insulated lunch cooler.

?

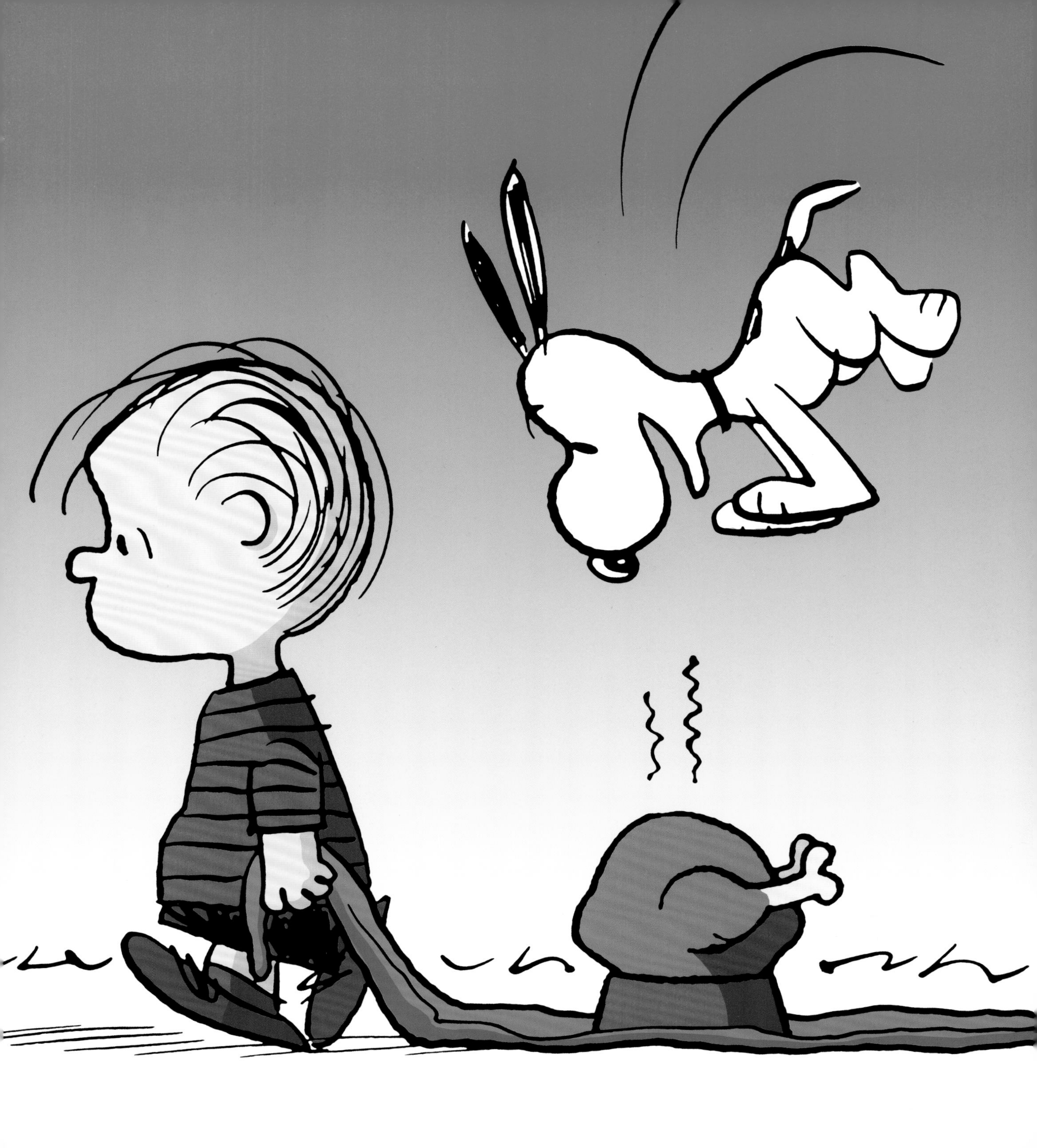

..AND A LITTLE MUSTARD, PLEASE.. THANK YOU...
I THINK I'LL HAVE THE "PLOUGHMAN'S LUNCH"
© 1990 United Feature Syndicate, Inc.
A HUNK OF BREAD, A SLAB OF CHEESE, A PICKLED ONION, A TOMATO AND A LETTUCE LEAF...
7-20
SO WHAT DO I GET? A HOT DOG!
SCHULZ

FARMER WOODSTOCK'S PLOUGHMAN'S LUNCH

Plough through the old-fashioned goodness of a lunchtime classic. The "ploughman's lunch," an English tradition dating back to the fourteenth century, began when farmworkers brought their lunch into the fields.

INGREDIENTS

1–2 tablespoons chutney
1 crusty bread roll or ¼ baguette, split
2 oz sliced ham
4 slices dill pickles
1 oz sliced Cheddar cheese
1 hard-boiled egg, peeled and chopped (page 23)
1 tablespoon Dijon mustard

Makes 1 sandwich

1 Spread the chutney on the bottom half of the roll. Lay the ham on top of the chutney, top with pickles, then the cheese. Arrange the chopped egg on top. Spread the mustard on the face of the top half of the roll, then place the roll on top of the chopped egg.

2 Wrap the sandwich in aluminum foil or place in an airtight container and close tightly. Refrigerate until ready to go, then pack in an insulated lunch cooler.

BEEP!
BEEP!

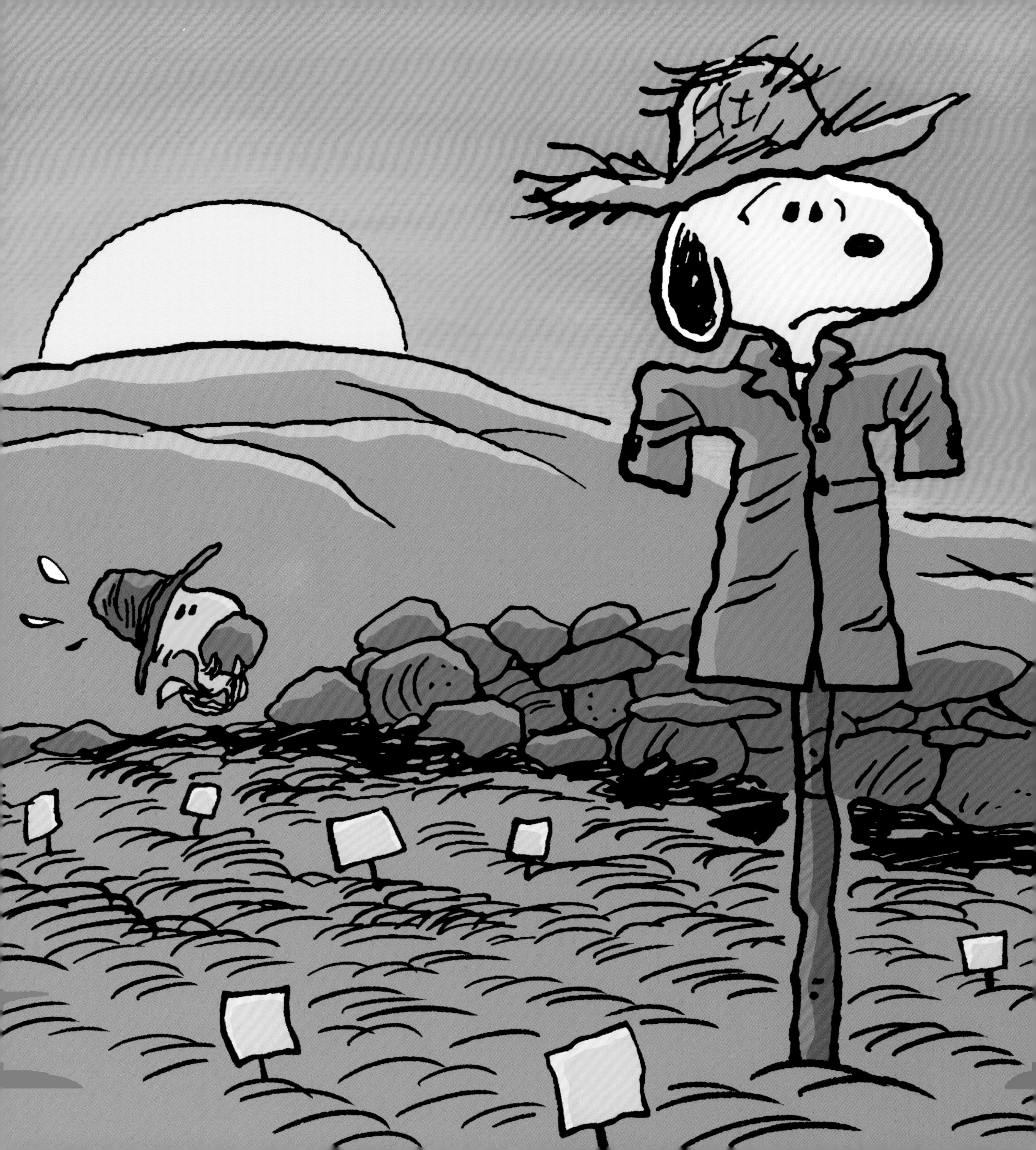

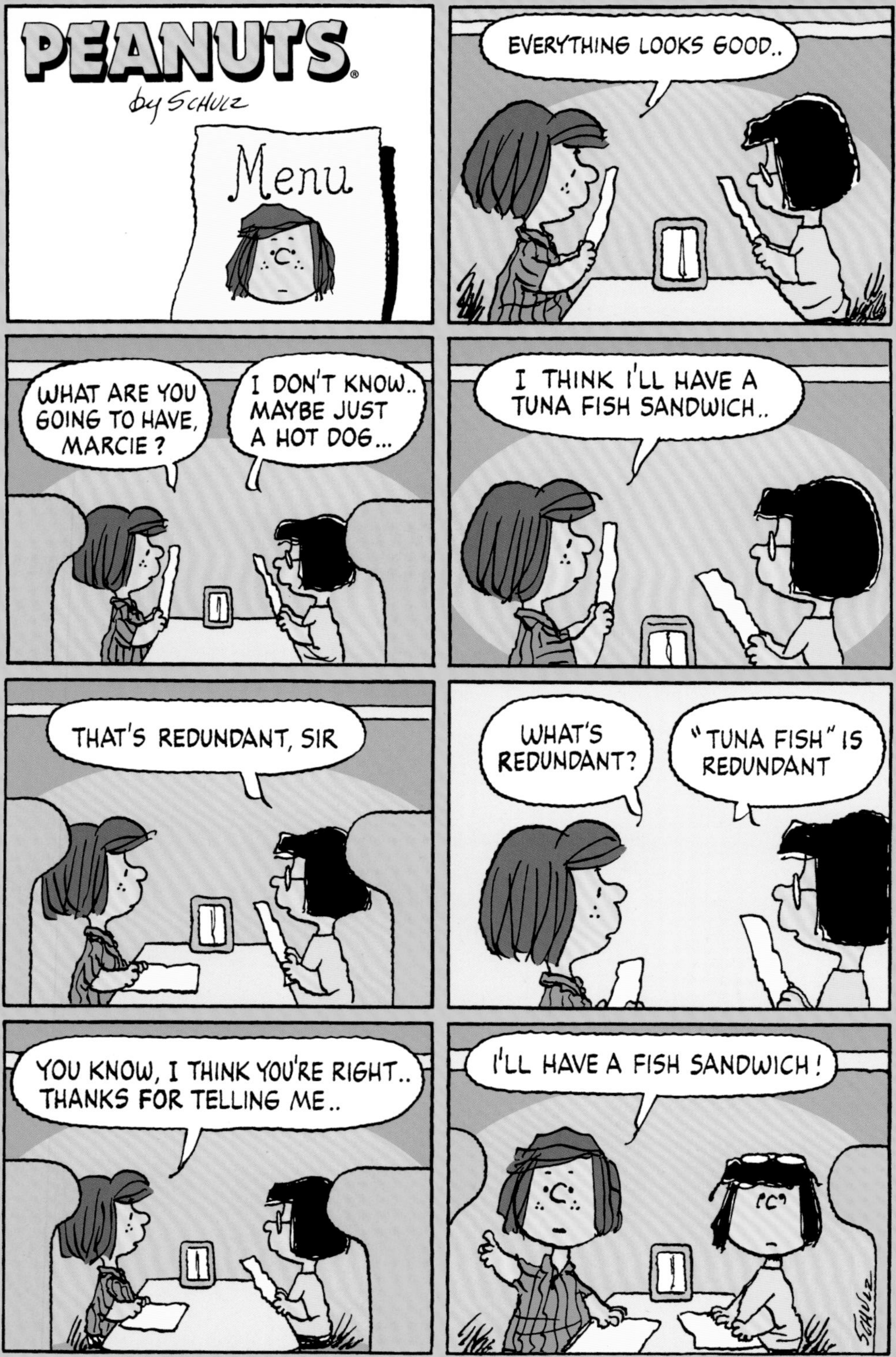
PEANUTS
by SCHULZ
Menu
EVERYTHING LOOKS GOOD..
WHAT ARE YOU GOING TO HAVE, MARCIE ?
I DON'T KNOW.. MAYBE JUST A HOT DOG...
I THINK I'LL HAVE A TUNA FISH SANDWICH..
THAT'S REDUNDANT, SIR
WHAT'S REDUNDANT?
"TUNA FISH" IS REDUNDANT
YOU KNOW, I THINK YOU'RE RIGHT.. THANKS FOR TELLING ME..
I'LL HAVE A FISH SANDWICH !
SCHULZ

...AND AN APPLE AND SOME CARROTS..
WHAT DO YOU HAVE?
A TUNA FLAT SANDWICH..
© 1987 United Feature Syndicate, Inc.
10-19
THE SCHOOL BUS RAN OVER MY LUNCH BOX!
SCHULZ

TUNA-IS-A-FISH SANDWICH

No matter how you ask for it, this tasty lunchtime standby will boost your brain power and energy with the omega-3 fat and protein found in tuna.

INGREDIENTS

1 can (6 oz) white albacore tuna, drained

2 tablespoons finely diced celery or bell pepper

1 tablespoon minced fresh flat-leaf parsley

2 teaspoons fresh lemon juice

1 tablespoon sweet pickle relish or chopped capers (optional)

1–2 tablespoons mayonnaise

4 thin slices sourdough, whole wheat, or white bread, toasted

Makes 2 sandwiches

1 In a bowl, combine the tuna, celery, parsley, lemon juice, pickle relish, if using, and just enough mayonnaise to bind it all together. Toss with a fork until well mixed. Pile the tuna mixture on 2 of the bread slices, dividing it evenly, then top with the remaining slices. Press gently.

2 Wrap each sandwich in aluminum foil or arrange in an airtight container and close tightly. Refrigerate until ready to go, then pack in an insulated lunch cooler.

I JUST SAW SOMETHING I'D LIKE TO HAVE FOR SCHOOL... A FIVE HUNDRED DOLLAR LUNCH BOX!
FIVE HUNDRED DOLLARS?!
© 1978 United Feature Syndicate, Inc.
THAT'S A LOT OF MONEY TO PAY FOR A LUNCH BOX
BUT WOULDN'T THE SANDWICHES TASTE GREAT?

BRING HOME THE BACON, LETTUCE & TOMATO WRAP

Even the humblest of lunch boxes will be enriched by this unique take on the standard BLT. Wrapping all this flavor in a flour tortilla is a million-dollar idea!

INGREDIENTS

2 slices applewood-smoked bacon

2 tablespoons mayonnaise

1 flour tortilla

¼ cup chopped romaine lettuce

¼ cup chopped tomato

Makes 1 wrap

1 In a frying pan, fry the bacon over medium heat, turning once, until crisp, 8–10 minutes. Transfer to paper towels to drain.

2 Spread the mayonnaise on the tortilla. Lay the bacon horizontally across the center of the tortilla. Top the bacon with chopped romaine lettuce and chopped tomato. Fold the right side of the tortilla partially over the filling, then roll up from the bottom into a tight cylinder (the filling will peek out the other side).

3 Wrap the sandwich in aluminum foil or place in an airtight container and close tightly. Refrigerate until ready to go, then pack in an insulated lunch cooler.

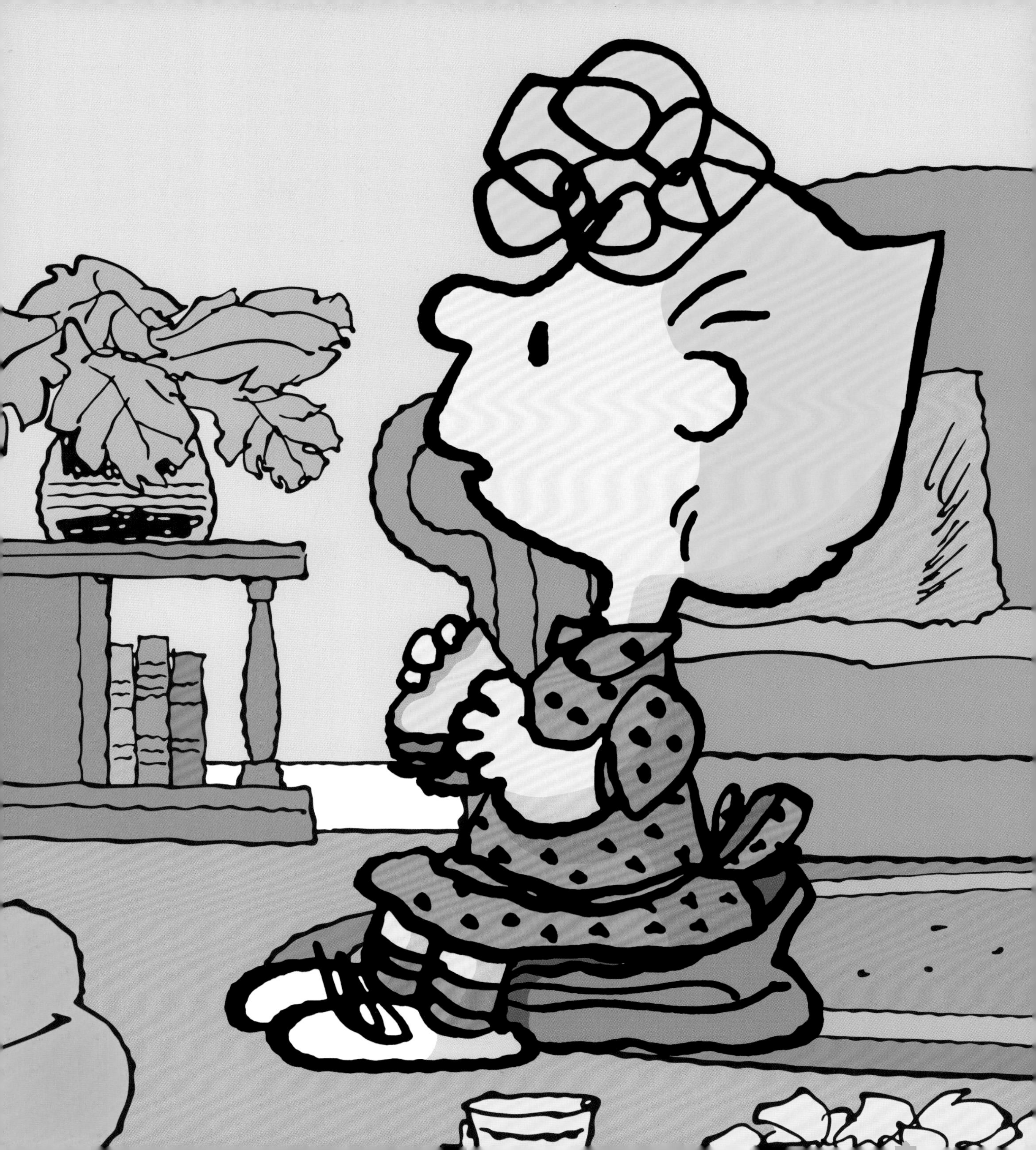

PEANUTS
SNIFF?
Tm. Reg. U. S. Pat Off.—All rights reserved Copr. 1957 by United Feature Syndicate, Inc.
WELL, HOW WAS THE BUTTERMILK?
SCHULZ
11-12

BETTER BUTTERMILK BISCUIT SANDWICHES

The fluffy, buttery richness of these made-from-scratch buttermilk biscuit sandwiches will please even the pickiest eater.

INGREDIENTS

1 cup all-purpose flour, plus more as needed
1 tablespoon firmly packed brown sugar
1 teaspoon baking powder
¼ teaspoon baking soda
Pinch of salt
3 tablespoons cold unsalted butter, cut into small pieces
6 tablespoons buttermilk
Mustard or mayonnaise (optional)
6 slices Cheddar cheese
6 slices Black Forest ham

Makes 6 biscuit sandwiches

1 Preheat the oven to 450°F. Line a rimmed baking sheet with parchment paper.

2 In a large bowl, stir together the flour, brown sugar, baking powder, baking soda, and salt. Using your fingertips, rub the butter into the flour mixture until it looks like coarse crumbs, with some chunks the size of peas. Add the buttermilk and stir until the dough starts to come together.

3 Transfer the dough to a lightly floured work surface and press it into a rough ball, then flatten it into a disk. Using a rolling pin, roll out the dough, sprinkling the dough and work surface with flour as needed to prevent sticking, to a thickness of about ½ inch. Using a 3-inch cookie or biscuit cutter, cut out as many biscuits as possible and place on the prepared baking sheet, spaced evenly apart. Gather up the scraps, press together, roll out, cut out more biscuits, and add them to the baking sheet. You should have 6 biscuits.

4 Bake until golden, 12–15 minutes. Transfer to a wire rack and let cool briefly. To make each sandwich, split open a biscuit with your hands. Slather one half with mustard or mayonnaise, if using. Layer 1 slice of the Cheddar on the biscuit half. Fold 1 slice of the ham over the cheese, then top with the other biscuit half.

5 Wrap each sandwich in aluminum foil or arrange in an airtight container and close tightly. Refrigerate until ready to go, then pack in an insulated lunch cooler.

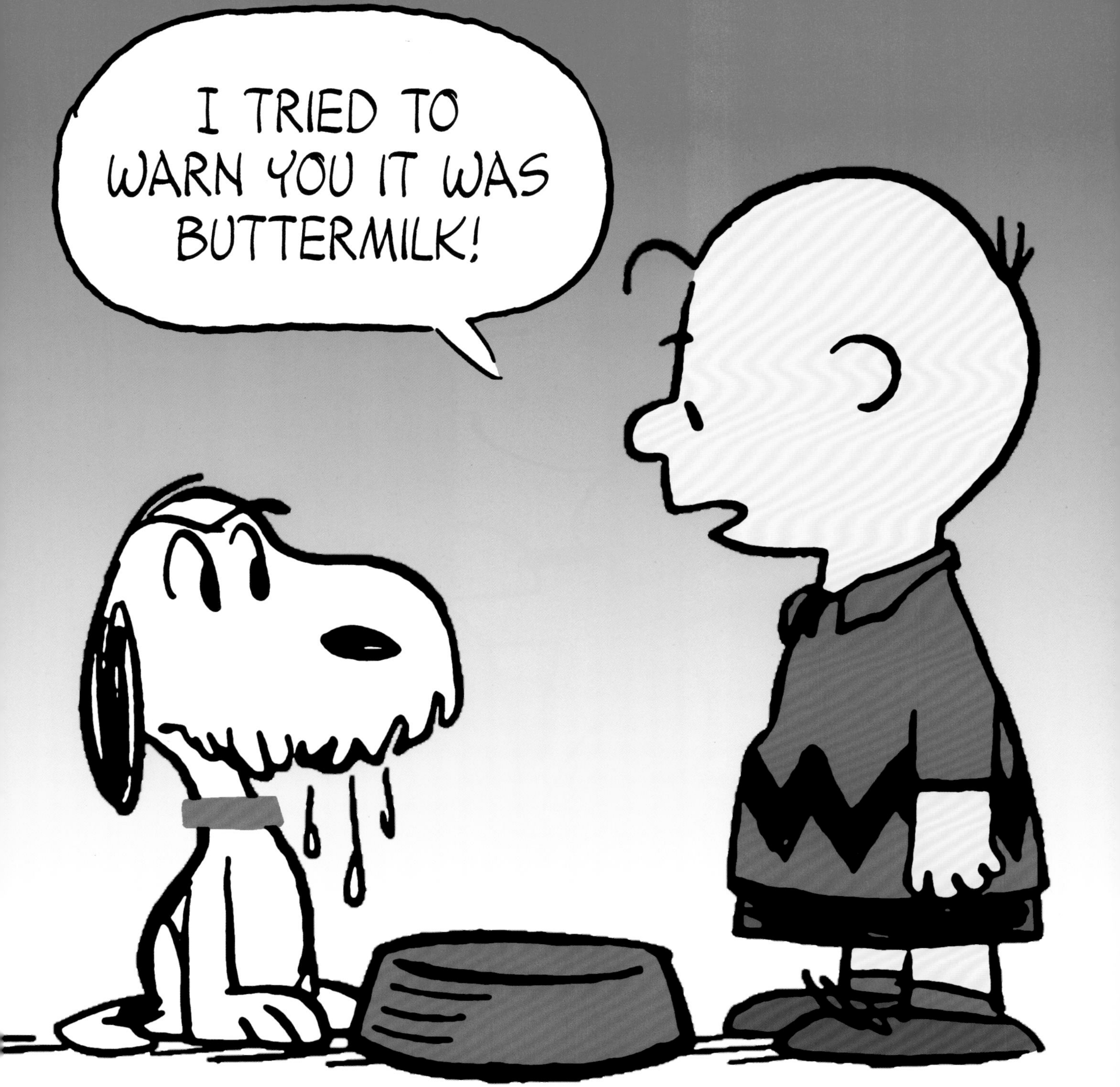
I TRIED TO WARN YOU IT WAS BUTTERMILK!

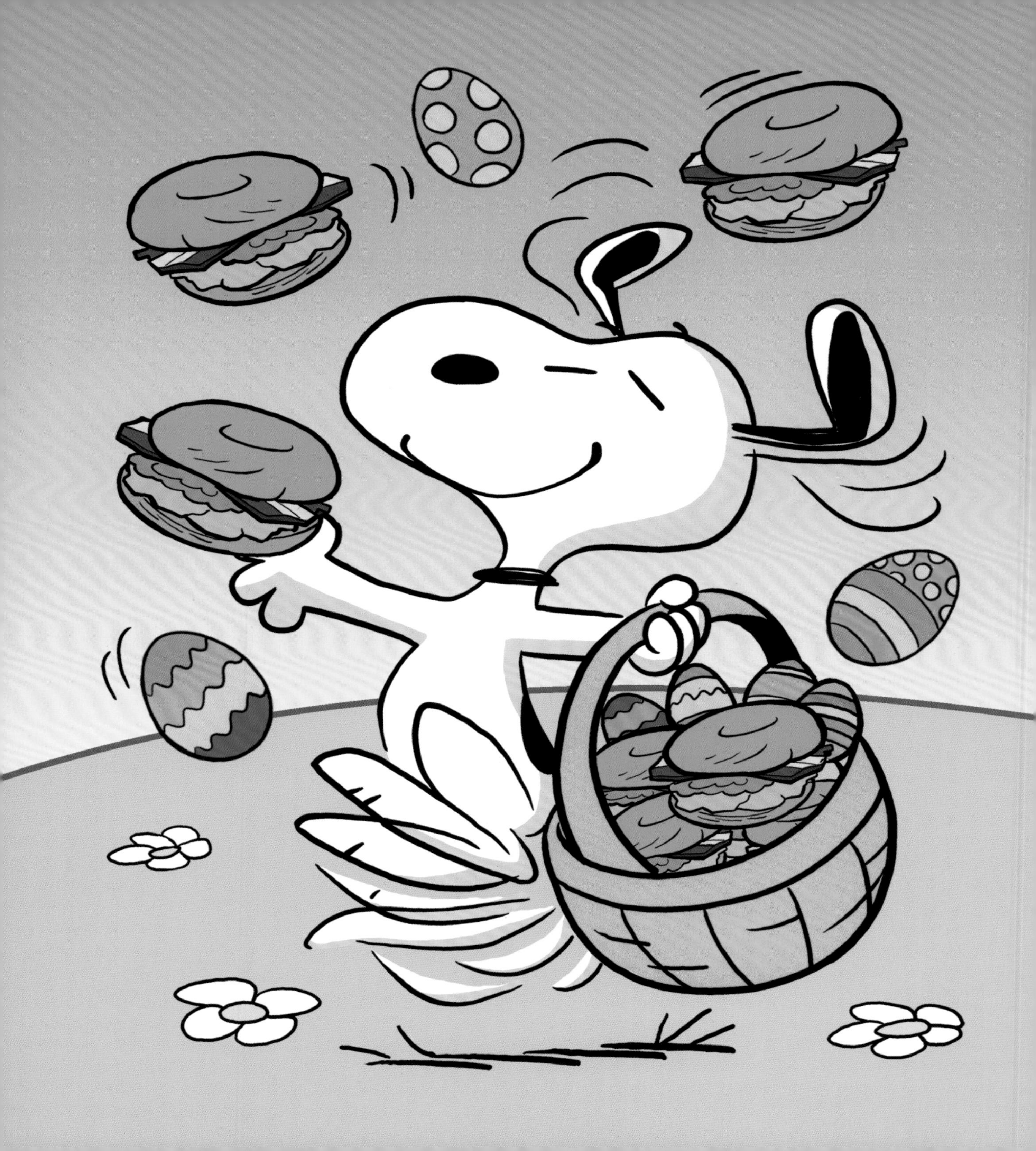

WHAT'S HE DOING IN HERE?
IT'S RAINING SO I THOUGHT HE MIGHT PREFER TO EAT INDOORS..
I'M SUPPOSED TO EAT AT THE SAME TABLE WITH A DOG?
10-14
THIS IS MY BREAD PLATE..YOUR BREAD PLATE IS THE ONE ON THE LEFT..
SCHULZ
www.unitedmedia.com
© 1996 United Feature Syndicate, Inc.

EGGSELLENT EASTER BEAGLE MINI BAGELS

These kid-size mini bagels paired with flavorful egg salad are a favorite any time of year!

INGREDIENTS

2 large eggs
1–2 tablespoons mayonnaise
1 teaspoon yellow mustard
Salt and freshly ground pepper
1 tablespoon minced fresh dill or flat-leaf parsley (optional)
2 mini bagels, split
6 thin slices cucumber

Makes 2 mini sandwiches

1 Put the eggs in a small saucepan and add cold water to cover. Bring to a boil over high heat, then reduce the heat to medium-low and simmer the eggs for 12 minutes. Place the saucepan in the sink and run cold water over the eggs to cool them. Roll each egg on a work surface to crack the eggshell. Carefully peel the shell.

2 Put the eggs in a bowl. Using a fork, mash the eggs against the bottom and sides of the bowl until small chunks form. Toss with just enough mayonnaise to bind the eggs together, then add the mustard. Mix until blended and a little creamy. Season to taste with salt and pepper. Stir in the parsley, if using.

3 Lightly toast the bagels. Pile the egg salad onto the bagel bottoms and top each with 3 cucumber slices. Cover with the bagel tops and press gently. (You will have some extra egg salad; use for additional sandwiches or as a snack with crackers later in the week.)

4 Wrap each sandwich in aluminum foil or arrange in an airtight container and close tightly. Refrigerate until ready to go, then pack in an insulated lunch cooler.

PEANUTS
WHAT'S YOUR DOG DOING DOWN AT THE PLAYGROUND, CHARLIE BROWN?
THE PLAYGROUND?
HERE I AM CARRYING OUT MY SPECIAL ASSIGNMENT FOR THE HEAD BEAGLE...
I'LL BE ON DUTY HERE ALL WEEK
WHENEVER YOU SEE A DOG ON A SCHOOL PLAYGROUND, YOU KNOW THAT HE HAS BEEN PLACED THERE BY ORDER OF THE HEAD BEAGLE!

PLAYGROUND SLIDERS

Slide into the deliciousness of mini pulled-chicken sandwiches served with fresh, tangy apple-jicama relish. Prepare this recipe for a family-size meal and you'll have plenty of leftovers to make the sliders.

INGREDIENTS

1 whole chicken, about 3½ lb
½ lemon
2 bay leaves
2 teaspoons salt
1 teaspoon freshly ground pepper
1 cup tomato purée
1 cup Dijon mustard
¾ cup apple cider vinegar
3 tablespoons firmly packed golden brown sugar
2 cloves garlic, minced
3 dashes hot-pepper sauce
Apple-Jicama Relish (page 118)
12 small soft rolls

Makes 12 sliders

1 In a large, heavy pot, combine the chicken, lemon half, bay leaves, 1 teaspoon of the salt, and ½ teaspoon of the pepper. Pour in enough water to cover the chicken and bring to a boil over high heat. Reduce the heat to medium-low and simmer until the chicken is cooked through, about 1 hour. Carefully remove the chicken from the pan and set aside to cool (discard the lemon and bay leaves). When the chicken is cool enough to handle, remove the meat, discarding the skin and bones. Shred the chicken into a large bowl.

2 Meanwhile, in a small saucepan, combine the tomato purée, mustard, vinegar, brown sugar, garlic, hot sauce, remaining 1 teaspoon salt, and remaining ½ teaspoon pepper. Set over high heat and bring to a boil. Reduce the heat to low and simmer until the flavors come together and the color deepens, about 25 minutes. Taste and season with additional salt and pepper if desired. Cool slightly, then pour over the shredded chicken. Stir to mix.

3 Spoon the chicken mixture and relish into separate airtight containers and close tightly. Refrigerate until ready to go, then pack the containers and rolls in an insulated lunch cooler. Store any leftover chicken in an airtight container in the refrigerator for up to 5 days.

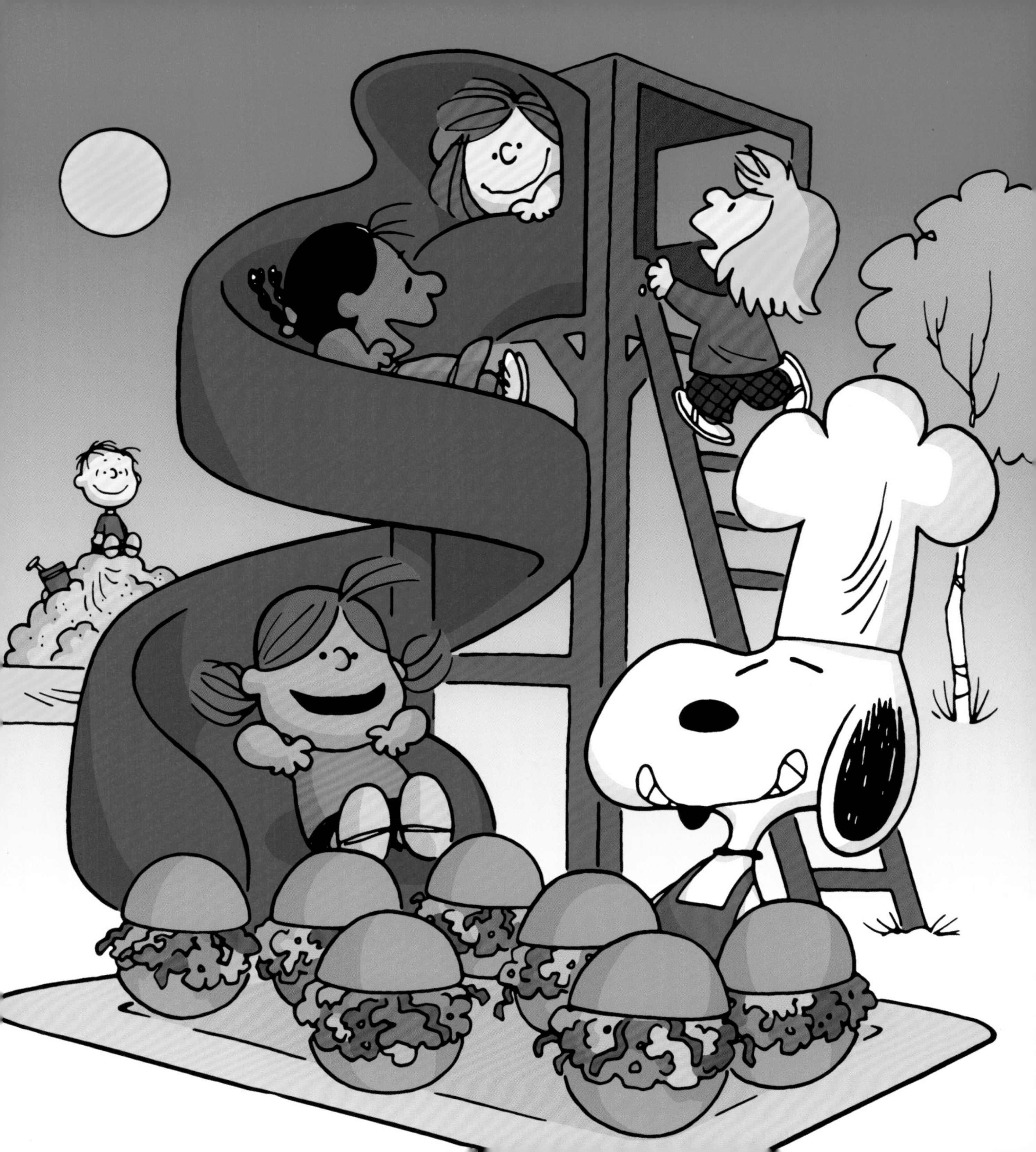

"PEANUTS"
DO YOU HAVE MUD-PIE SANDWICHES TO TAKE OUT?
YES, WE DO...WOULD LIKE YOURS 'WITH' OR 'WITHOUT'?
'WITH' OR 'WITHOUT' WHAT? ONIONS?
NO...CRABGRASS!

VIOLET'S VEGGIE BITES

These tasty deconstructed "sandwiches"—a combination of veggies and beans rolled in bread crumbs and baked—pack a delight in every bite.

INGREDIENTS

FOR THE VEGGIE BITES:

½ cup quinoa, rinsed
1 cup water or reduced-sodium chicken broth
1¾ teaspoons salt
1 tablespoon olive oil
½ yellow onion, diced
½ lb cremini or other brown mushrooms, brushed clean, stemmed, and sliced
2 cups cauliflower florets
1 carrot, peeled and coarsely chopped
1 cup packed baby spinach
½ cup lightly packed fresh cilantro or flat-leaf parsley

1 To make the veggie bites, in a saucepan, bring the quinoa, water, and ¼ teaspoon of the salt to a boil over high heat. Reduce the heat to low, give the quinoa a stir, cover, and cook, without lifting the lid, until the liquid is absorbed and the quinoa is tender, about 15 minutes. Remove from the heat and let stand, covered, for 5 minutes. Uncover and fluff with a fork.

2 Meanwhile, in a large frying pan, warm the oil over medium heat. Add the onion and cook, stirring occasionally, until starting to sweat, about 2 minutes. Add the mushrooms and cook, stirring occasionally, until golden brown, about 4 minutes longer. (As the mushrooms start to release water, use it to help you scrape up the browned bits on the bottom of the pan.) Remove from the heat and let cool.

3 Put the cauliflower in a food processor and pulse a few times, until it starts to resemble rice. Add the onion-mushroom mixture, carrot, spinach, cilantro, black beans, tomato paste, chili powder, paprika, remaining 1½ teaspoons salt, and pepper and pulse a few times to mix well. Add the eggs and pulse just until combined. Transfer the mixture to a large bowl. Add ½ cup of the bread crumbs and the quinoa and, using a silicone spatula, stir until well mixed. Cover and refrigerate until the mixture becomes firm enough to shape, about 30 minutes.

1 can (15 oz) black beans, drained, rinsed, and patted dry with a paper towel
1 tablespoon tomato paste
2 teaspoons chili powder
1½ teaspoons smoked paprika
½ teaspoon freshly ground pepper
2 large eggs, lightly beaten
1½ cups panko bread crumbs

FOR THE YOGURT-TAHINI SAUCE:
1 cup plain whole-milk Greek yogurt
2 tablespoons tahini
1 clove garlic, minced
1 tablespoon fresh lemon juice
1 teaspoon salt
¼ teaspoon freshly ground pepper
1 teaspoon hot-pepper sauce such as Sriracha or Tabasco, or to taste (optional)

Makes about 42 bites

4 While the veggie bite mixture chills, make the sauce. In a bowl, combine the yogurt, tahini, garlic, lemon juice, salt, pepper, and hot sauce, if using, and stir until well blended. Taste and add more lemon juice, salt, and pepper if needed. Transfer to an airtight container and close tightly. Refrigerate until ready to go.

5 Preheat the oven to 400°F. Line 2 rimmed baking sheets with parchment paper. Spread the remaining 1 cup bread crumbs on a plate. Using a small ice-cream scoop or a tablespoon, scoop up a little of the veggie bite mixture, forming it into a ball. Toss and roll the ball in the bread crumbs, coating evenly, then place on a prepared baking sheet. Repeat with the remaining mixture, spacing the balls evenly apart.

6 Bake until golden brown and firm, 35–40 minutes. Let cool slightly on the pans on wire racks. Transfer to an airtight container and close tightly. Refrigerate until ready to go, then pack along with the sauce in an insulated lunch cooler. Store any leftover bites in an airtight container in the refrigerator for up to 5 days.

UGH, MARCIE! HOW CAN YOU EAT THAT?
IT'S NOT NICE, SIR, TO MAKE DISPARAGING REMARKS ABOUT WHAT SOMEONE IS EATING!
© 1989 United Feature Syndicate, Inc.
ACTUALLY, IF YOU CAN'T SAY SOMETHING NICE, YOU SHOULDN'T SAY ANYTHING AT ALL...
11-17
YOU HAVE A CUTE LUNCH, MARCIE..
SCHULZ

MARCIE'S VERY HEALTHY™ CHEESE & SPROUTS SANDWICH

Create your own brand of healthy goodness by giving your little sprout a lunch that is big on flavor and nutrition.

INGREDIENTS

½ baguette, cut in half crosswise and split
¼ lb Brie cheese, softened
2 tablespoons Dijon mustard
1 bunch alfalfa sprouts

Makes 2 sandwiches

1 Spread the baguette bottoms with the softened Brie and the tops with Dijon mustard.

2 Place a handful of sprouts on top of the cheese. Cover with the baguette tops, mustard side down.

3 Wrap each sandwich in aluminum foil or arrange in an airtight container and close tightly. Refrigerate until ready to go, then pack in an insulated lunch cooler.

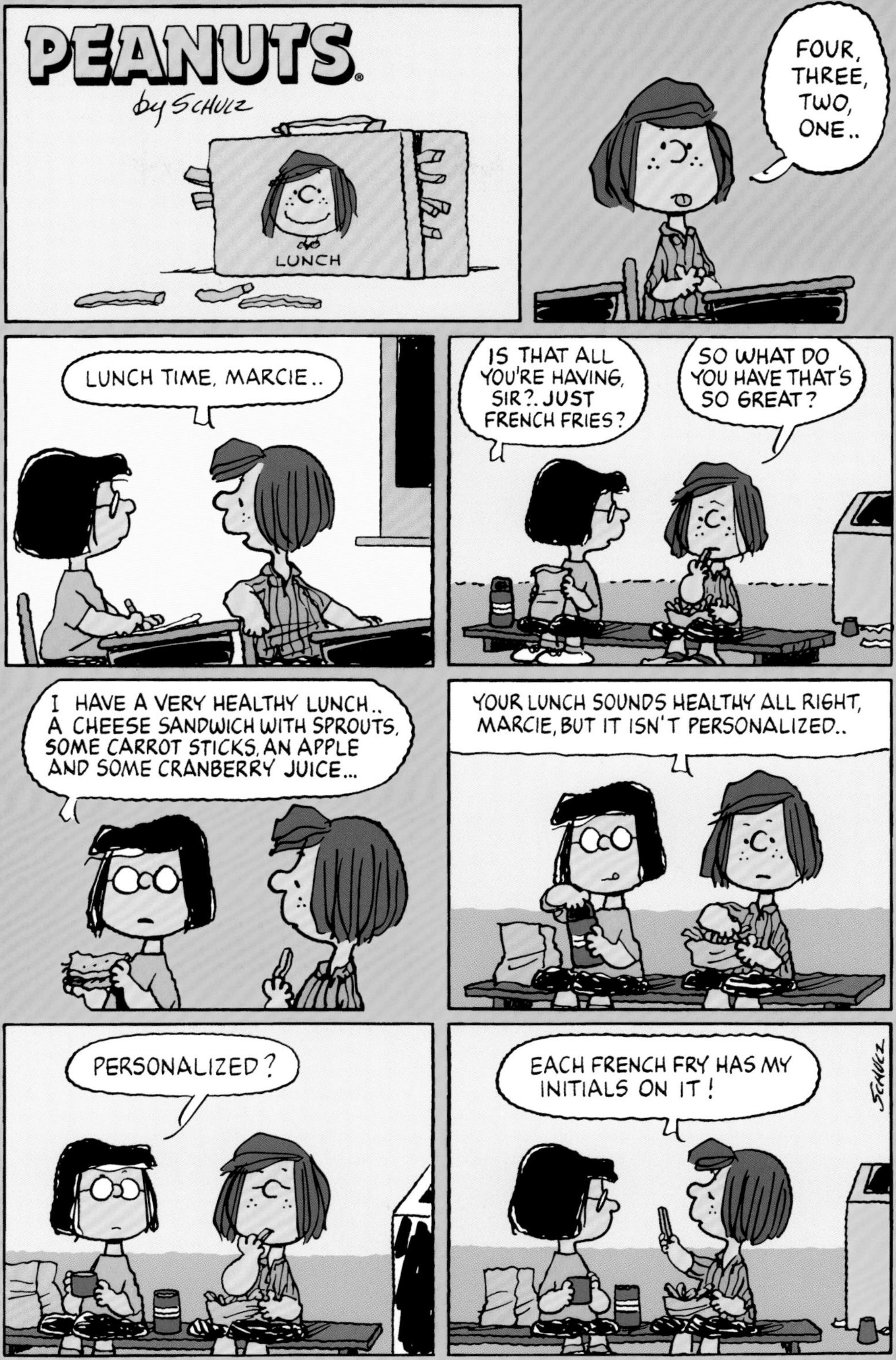
PEANUTS
by SCHULZ
LUNCH
FOUR, THREE, TWO, ONE..
LUNCH TIME, MARCIE..
IS THAT ALL YOU'RE HAVING, SIR?. JUST FRENCH FRIES?
SO WHAT DO YOU HAVE THAT'S SO GREAT?
I HAVE A VERY HEALTHY LUNCH.. A CHEESE SANDWICH WITH SPROUTS, SOME CARROT STICKS, AN APPLE AND SOME CRANBERRY JUICE...
YOUR LUNCH SOUNDS HEALTHY ALL RIGHT, MARCIE, BUT IT ISN'T PERSONALIZED..
PERSONALIZED?
EACH FRENCH FRY HAS MY INITIALS ON IT!
SCHULZ

I HOPE YOU WON'T MIND...
MIND WHAT?
© 1977 United Feature Syndicate, Inc.
WE'RE ALL OUT OF DOG FOOD SO I MADE YOU A SANDWICH
12-19
SCHULZ

SNOOPY'S DEEP-DIVE SUB

Dive into a classic submarine sandwich. Mix and match the ingredients—pile on all the flavors that float your boat!

INGREDIENTS

½ cup mayonnaise
Grated zest and juice of 1 lemon
1 clove garlic, minced
Pinch of kosher salt
1 baguette, split
¼ lb provolone cheese
½ lb thinly sliced ham
½ lb thinly sliced salami
⅓ lb thinly sliced coppa or soppressata
1 cup shredded lettuce
2 Roma tomatoes, sliced
⅓ cup sliced peperoncini
1 red bell pepper, seeded and sliced

Makes 6 small sandwiches

1 In a small bowl, whisk together the mayonnaise, lemon zest and juice, garlic, and salt. Slather the aioli on the cut sides of the baguette. On the bottom half, layer the cheese and meats, followed by the lettuce, tomatoes, peperoncini, and red bell pepper. Cover with the top half and cut into 6 sections.

2 Wrap each sandwich section in aluminum foil or arrange in an airtight container and close tightly. Refrigerate until ready to go, then pack in an insulated lunch cooler.

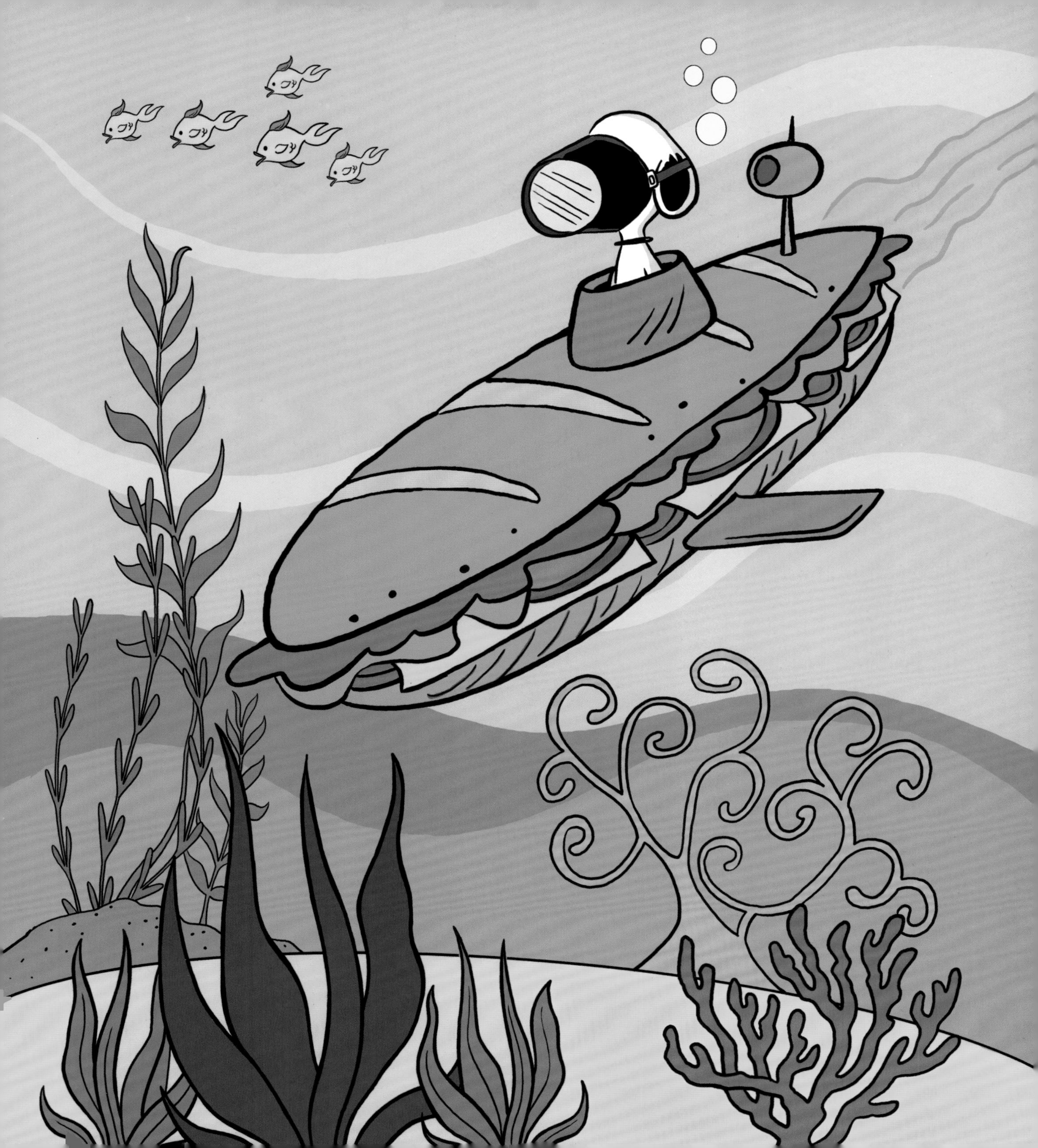

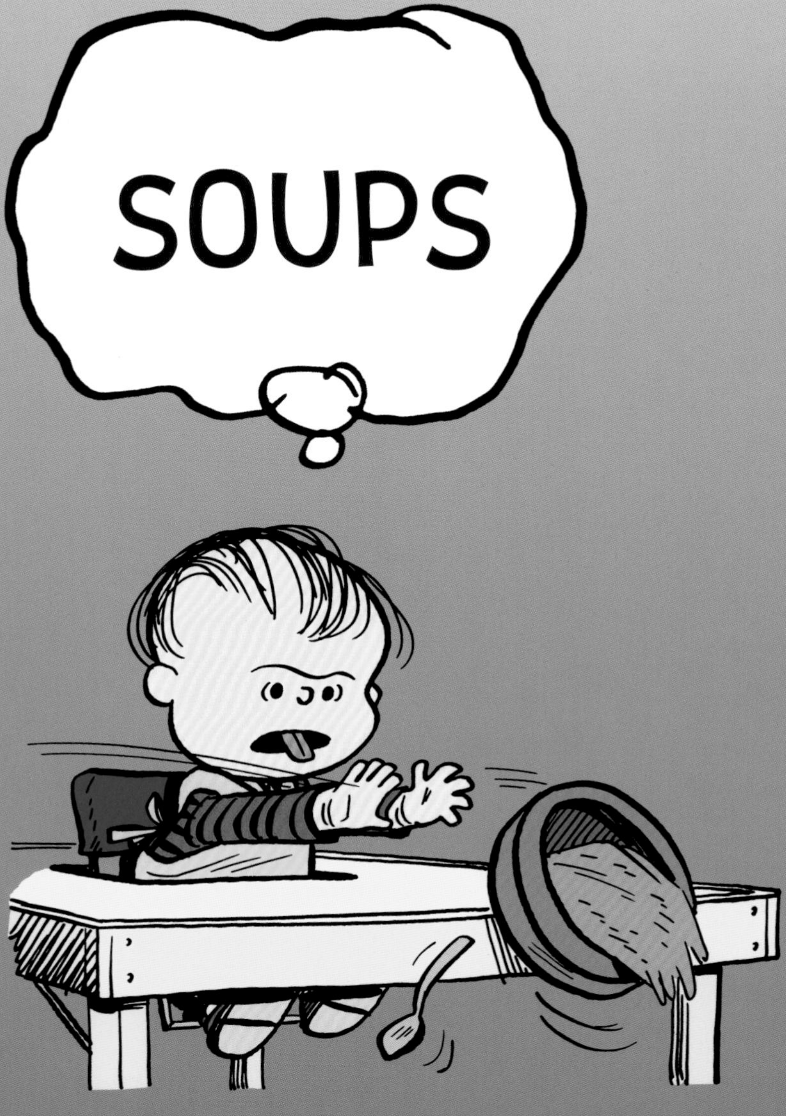
SOUPS

I'M FIXING YOUR DINNER RIGHT NOW..
WHILE YOU'RE WAITING, I THOUGHT YOU MIGHT LIKE SOME SOUP..AND WHILE YOU'RE WAITING FOR THE SOUP, I'LL BRING YOU SOME FRENCH BREAD..
7-23
AND WHILE YOU'RE WAITING FOR THE BREAD, I THOUGHT YOU MIGHT LIKE SOME CARROTS...
© 1988 United Feature Syndicate, Inc.
WHAT DO I EAT WHILE I'M WAITING FOR THE CARROTS?
SCHULZ

"BOWL" OF SPLIT PEA SOUP

You will be bowled over by the flavorful blend of sweet peas and salty bacon in this hearty and satisfying lunchtime standard.

INGREDIENTS

1 tablespoon olive oil
1 yellow onion, finely diced
1 rib celery, thinly sliced
2 small carrots, peeled and thinly sliced
1 cup dried green or yellow split peas, picked over and rinsed
4 cups reduced-sodium chicken or vegetable broth
6 slices bacon
2 tablespoons finely chopped fresh flat-leaf parsley
½ teaspoon finely chopped fresh marjoram
½ teaspoon finely chopped fresh thyme
Salt and freshly ground pepper

Makes 4 servings

1 In a large, heavy pot, warm the oil over medium heat. Add the onion and cook, stirring, until softened, 3–5 minutes. Add the celery and carrots and cook, stirring, just until slightly softened, about 3 minutes. Add the split peas, broth, 2 of the bacon slices, the parsley, marjoram, and thyme. Reduce the heat to medium-low and bring to a simmer. Cover partially and cook until the peas are tender, 50–60 minutes. Remove from the heat, discard the bacon, and let cool.

2 Meanwhile, in a frying pan, fry the remaining 4 bacon slices over medium heat, turning once, until crisp, 8–10 minutes. Transfer to paper towels to drain. Let cool, then crumble.

3 Coarsely purée 2 cups of the soup in a blender and return to the pot. Simmer the soup over medium heat for 5 minutes. Taste and season with salt and pepper.

4 Ladle servings of the soup into insulated containers, garnish with the crumbled bacon, and close tightly. Let any remaining soup cool, then cover tightly and refrigerate for up to 4 days or freeze individual portions for up to 4 months.

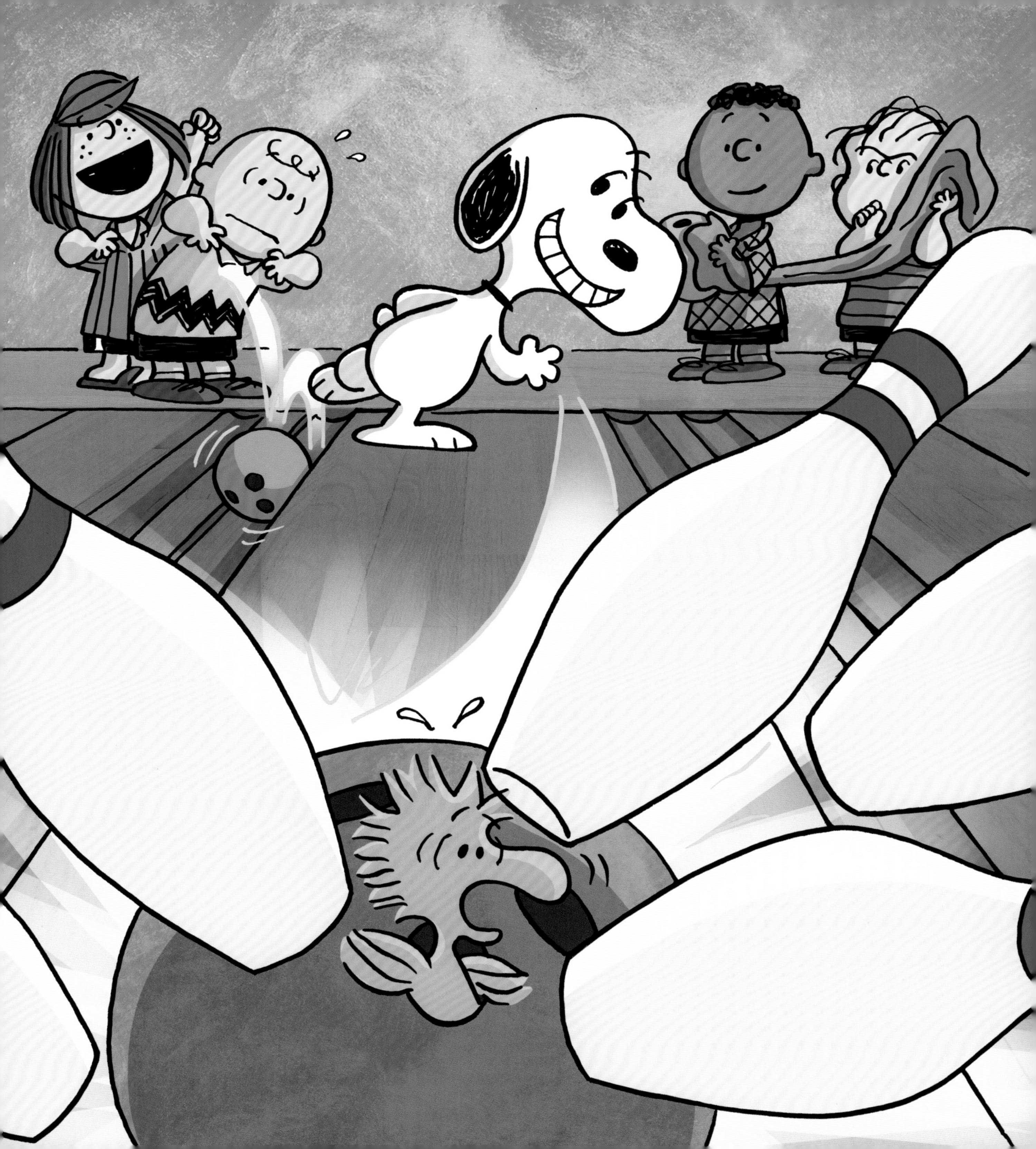

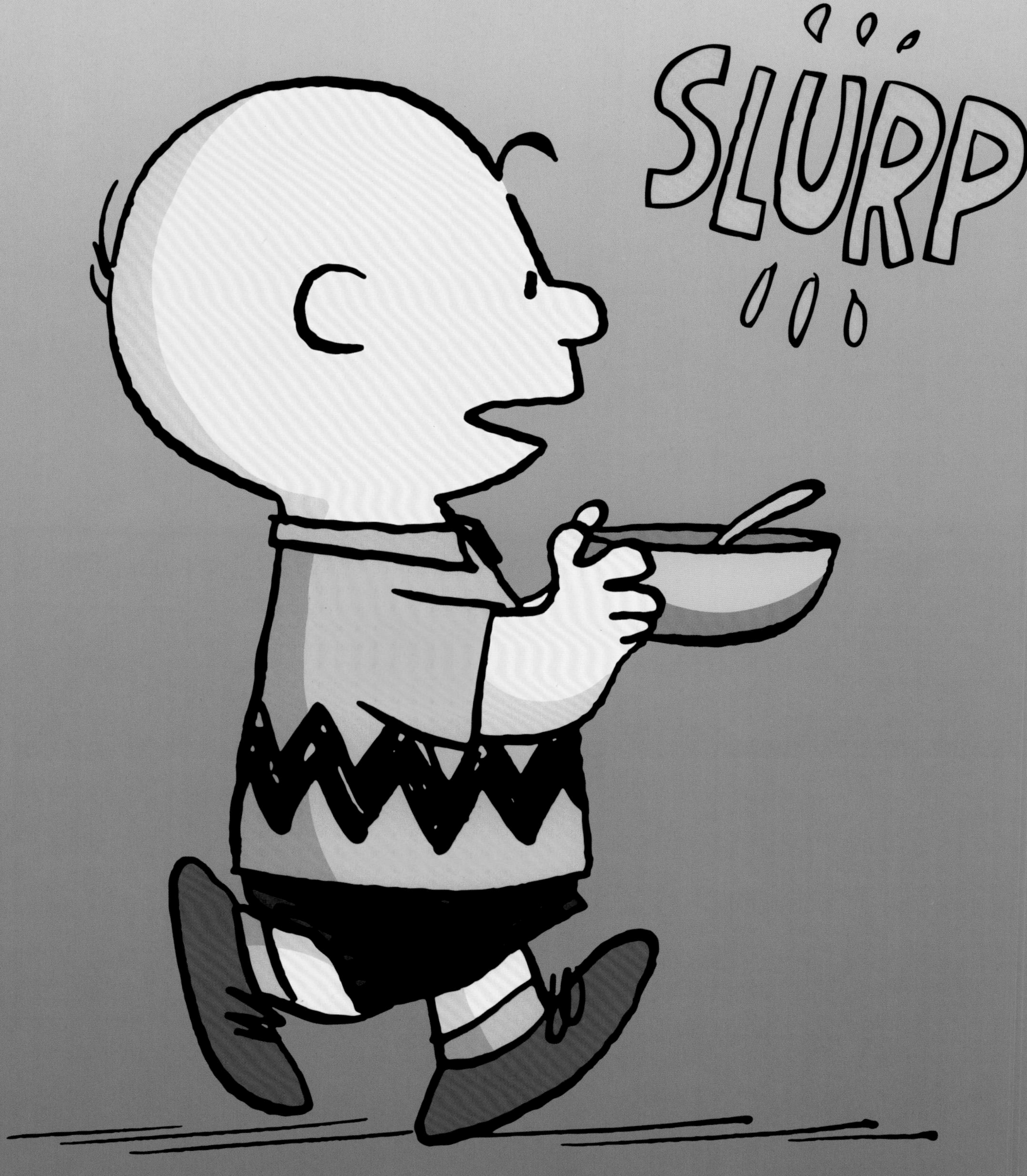
SLURP

"PEANUTS"
WELL, WE'RE ALL SET FOR OUR PICNIC...
HERE'S THE ICE CREAM!
AND HERE'S THE CAKE...
Copr. 1951 by United Feature Syndicate, Inc.
WHAT ARE YOU HOLDING IN YOUR HANDS, CHARLIE BROWN?
SOUP!
SCHULZ
8/3

CHARLIE BROWN'S HANDMADE CHICKEN & FARFALLE VEGETABLE SOUP

Share the wholesome nourishment of classic chicken-and-noodle soup.

INGREDIENTS

1 small chicken (about 3 lb), quartered and skinned
1 large yellow onion, coarsely chopped
1 carrot, peeled and coarsely chopped
6 sprigs fresh flat-leaf parsley, plus ¼ cup finely chopped parsley
1 teaspoon chopped fresh thyme
2 bay leaves
2½ quarts water
3 ribs celery with leaves, cut into ½-inch pieces
½ small head savoy cabbage, cored and coarsely chopped
½ lb green beans, trimmed and cut into 1-inch pieces
2 cups farfalle
1 tablespoon fresh lemon juice
Salt and freshly ground pepper
¾ cup grated Parmesan cheese

Makes 6 servings

1 In a large, heavy pot, combine the chicken, onion, carrot, parsley sprigs, thyme, and bay leaves. Pour in the water and bring to a boil over high heat. Reduce the heat to medium-low, cover, and simmer until the meat falls from the bones, about 1 hour.

2 Transfer the chicken to a plate. Strain the broth through a fine-mesh sieve and return to the pot. Once the chicken is cool enough to handle, remove the meat from the bones and discard the bones. Tear the meat into 1-inch pieces.

3 Add the celery, cabbage, green beans, and farfalle to the pot, cover, and simmer until the farfalle is al dente, 10–12 minutes or according to the package directions. Add the chicken pieces, chopped parsley, and lemon juice. Season to taste with salt and pepper. Cook, stirring occasionally, until the chicken is warmed through.

4 Ladle servings of the soup into insulated containers, top with the Parmesan, and close tightly. Let any remaining soup cool, then cover tightly and refrigerate for up to 4 days or freeze individual portions for up to 4 months.

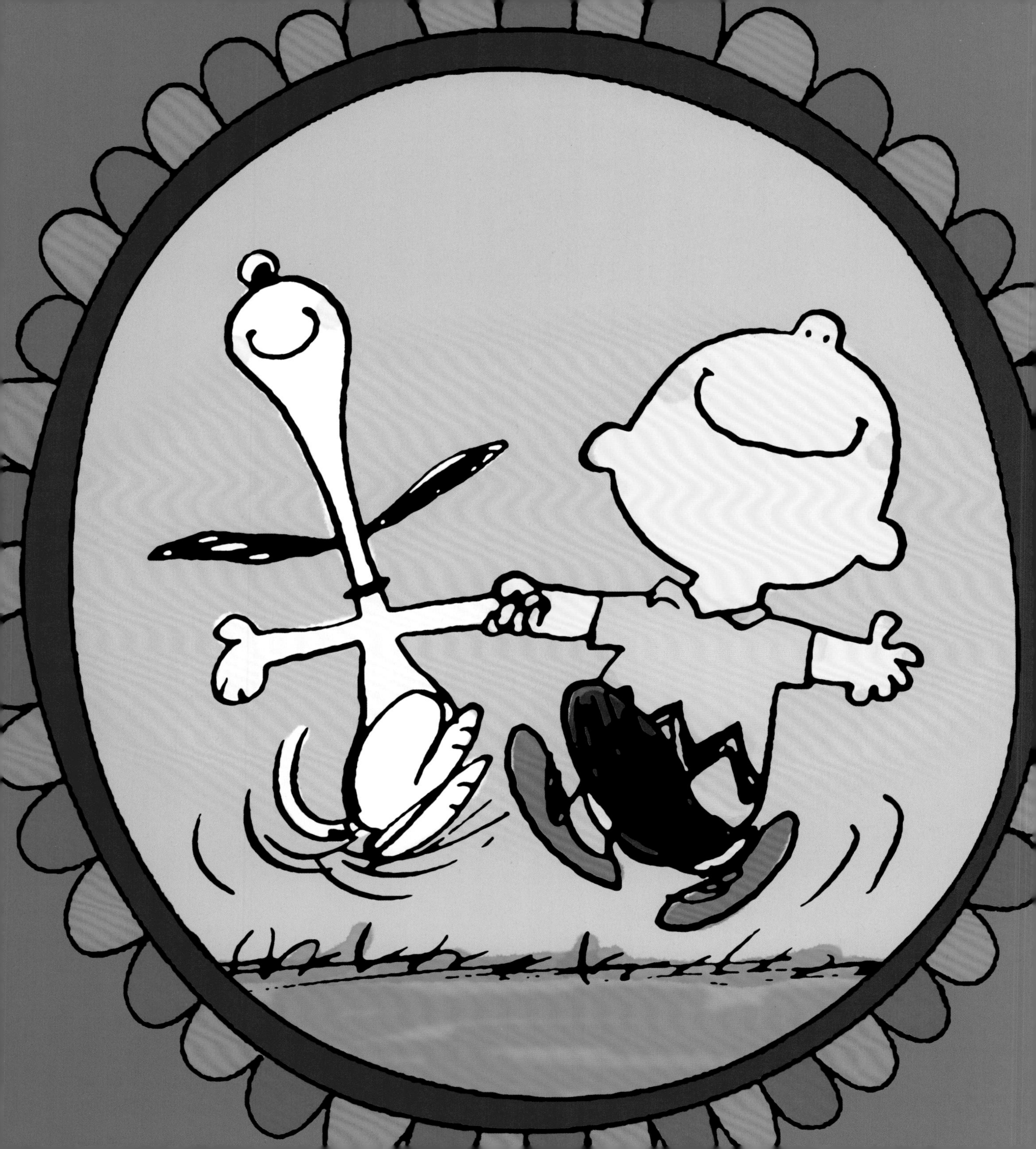

SURPRISE!
I'VE BROUGHT YOU SOME AUTHENTIC BIRD'S-NEST SOUP!
AUTHENTIC? HOW DO I KNOW IT'S AUTHENTIC?
© 1978 United Feature Syndicate, Inc.
4-14
SCHULZ

HAPPINESS IS . . . A BOWL OF TOMATO RICE SOUP

Your feet will do the happy dance once you sip the authentically scrumptious flavors of this creamy tomato soup—cozy comfort for any season.

INGREDIENTS

3 tablespoons unsalted butter
1 small yellow onion, chopped
2 cloves garlic, minced
2 cans (28 oz each) diced tomatoes with juices
¼ cup heavy cream
1 cup steamed white rice
Salt and freshly ground pepper

Makes 4 to 6 servings

1 In a large saucepan, melt the butter over medium-high heat. Add the onion and garlic and cook, stirring, until translucent, about 5 minutes. Add the tomatoes and their juices and bring to a boil. Reduce the heat to low and simmer for 20 minutes. Remove from the heat and let cool.

2 Working in batches, purée the soup in a blender. Return to the saucepan. Stir in the cream and rice and return to a gentle boil. Season to taste with salt and pepper.

3 Ladle servings of the soup into insulated containers and close tightly. Let any remaining soup cool, then cover tightly and refrigerate for up to 4 days.

OH, GREAT PUMPKIN, PLEASE DON'T LET ME DOWN!
10-31
VINDICATE ME BEFORE MINE ENEMIES! DELIVER ME FROM MY ADVERSARIES!!
SHOW UP, STUPID!!!

IT'S THE GREAT PUMPKIN SOUP!

A sip of this soothing soup, excellent for a cold autumn day, will ease the long wait for the Great Pumpkin.

INGREDIENTS

2 tablespoons unsalted butter
1 shallot, minced
2 cloves garlic, minced
¼ lb Gruyère or Swiss cheese, finely grated
2 cans (15 oz) pumpkin purée
Pinch of grated nutmeg
2 cups reduced-sodium chicken broth
2 tablespoons heavy cream
Salt and freshly ground pepper

Makes 4 to 6 servings

1 In a large, heavy pot, melt the butter over medium-high heat. Add the shallot and garlic and cook until very soft, 3–4 minutes. Add half of the Gruyère and stir until the cheese begins to melt. Stir in the pumpkin, nutmeg, and broth and bring to a boil. Reduce the heat to low and simmer for 15 minutes. Stir in the cream. Season to taste with salt and pepper.

2 Ladle servings of the soup into insulated containers, top with the remaining Gruyère, and close tightly. Let any remaining soup cool, then cover tightly and refrigerate for up to 4 days.

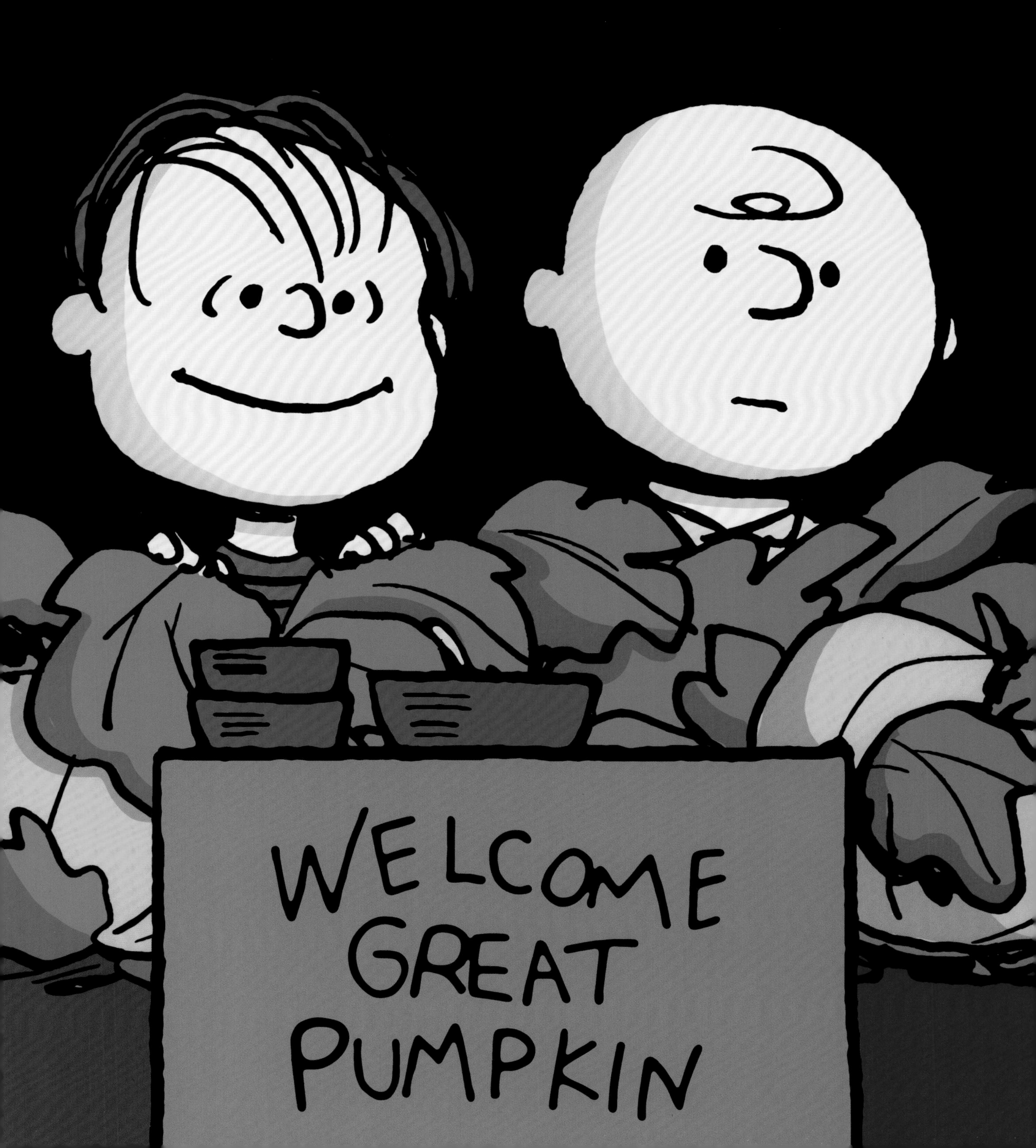
WELCOME
GREAT
PUMPKIN

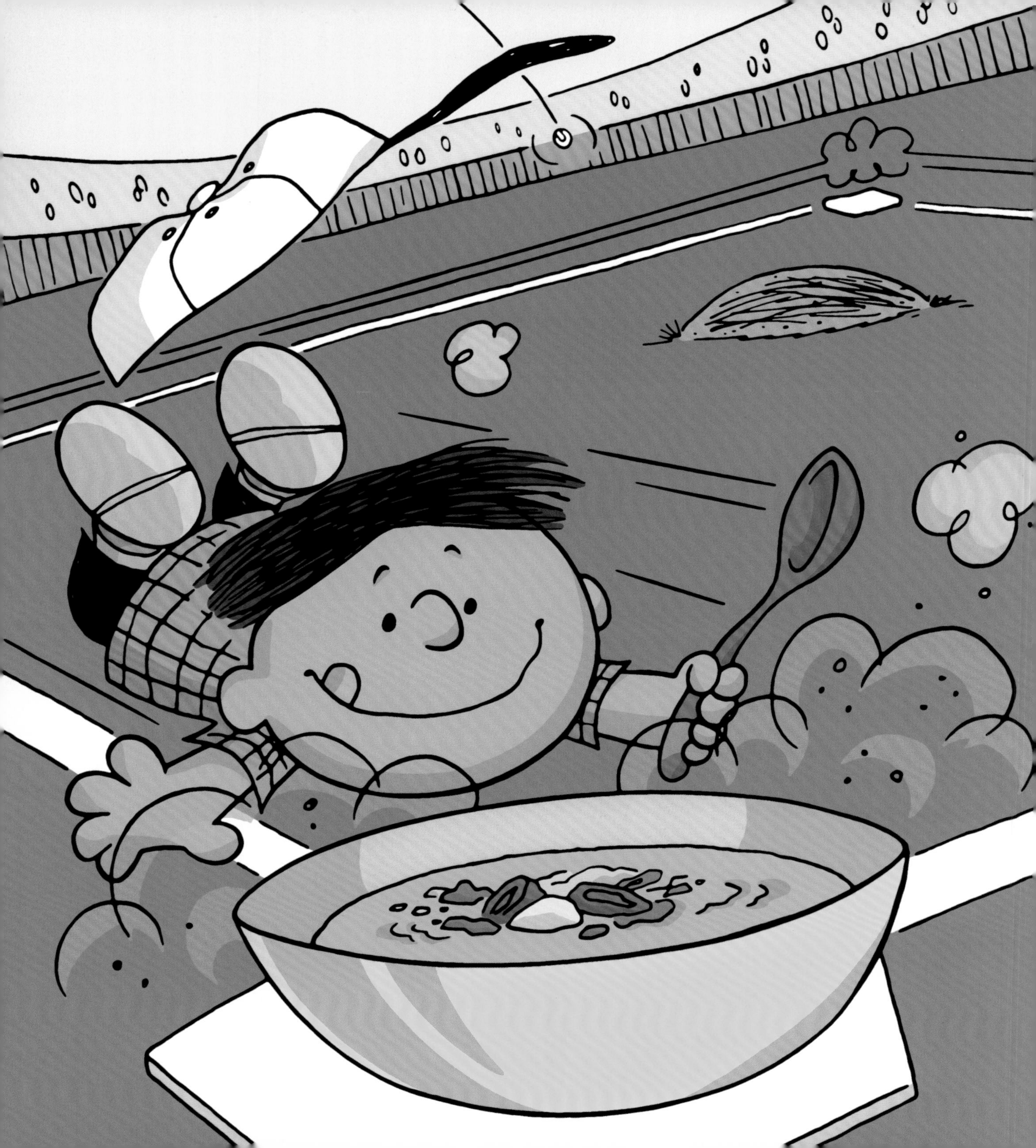

PEANUTS
HELLO?
HELLO, CHUCK? THIS IS OL' PEPPERMINT PATTY! HAVE I GOT A SURPRISE FOR YOU! I'VE FOUND YOU A NEW BALL PLAYER....
3-20
THIS GUY IS TERRIFIC! HE'S NOT VERY BIG, BUT HE CAN REALLY PLAY! HIS NAME?
JOSÉ PETERSON!
SCHULZ

JOSÉ PETERSON'S SPRING TRAINING SOUP

Cross home plate for avocado soup topped with shrimp and salsa. This recipe makes a family-size batch—it's best eaten fresh, so use the leftovers right away!

INGREDIENTS

3 large avocados, pitted, peeled, and coarsely chopped
3 cups reduced-sodium chicken broth
1 cup heavy cream
2 tablespoons fresh lemon juice
Salt and freshly ground pepper
12–16 large cooked shrimp, peeled, deveined, and diced
Fresh Tomato Salsa (page 118)

Makes 6 to 8 servings

1. To make the soup, working in batches, purée the avocados, broth, and cream in a blender. Transfer to a bowl. Add the lemon juice and season to taste with salt and pepper. Cover and refrigerate for 1 hour.

2. Ladle servings of the soup into insulated containers, top with the shrimp, garnish with the salsa, and close tightly. Let any remaining soup cool, then cover tightly and refrigerate for up to 1 day.

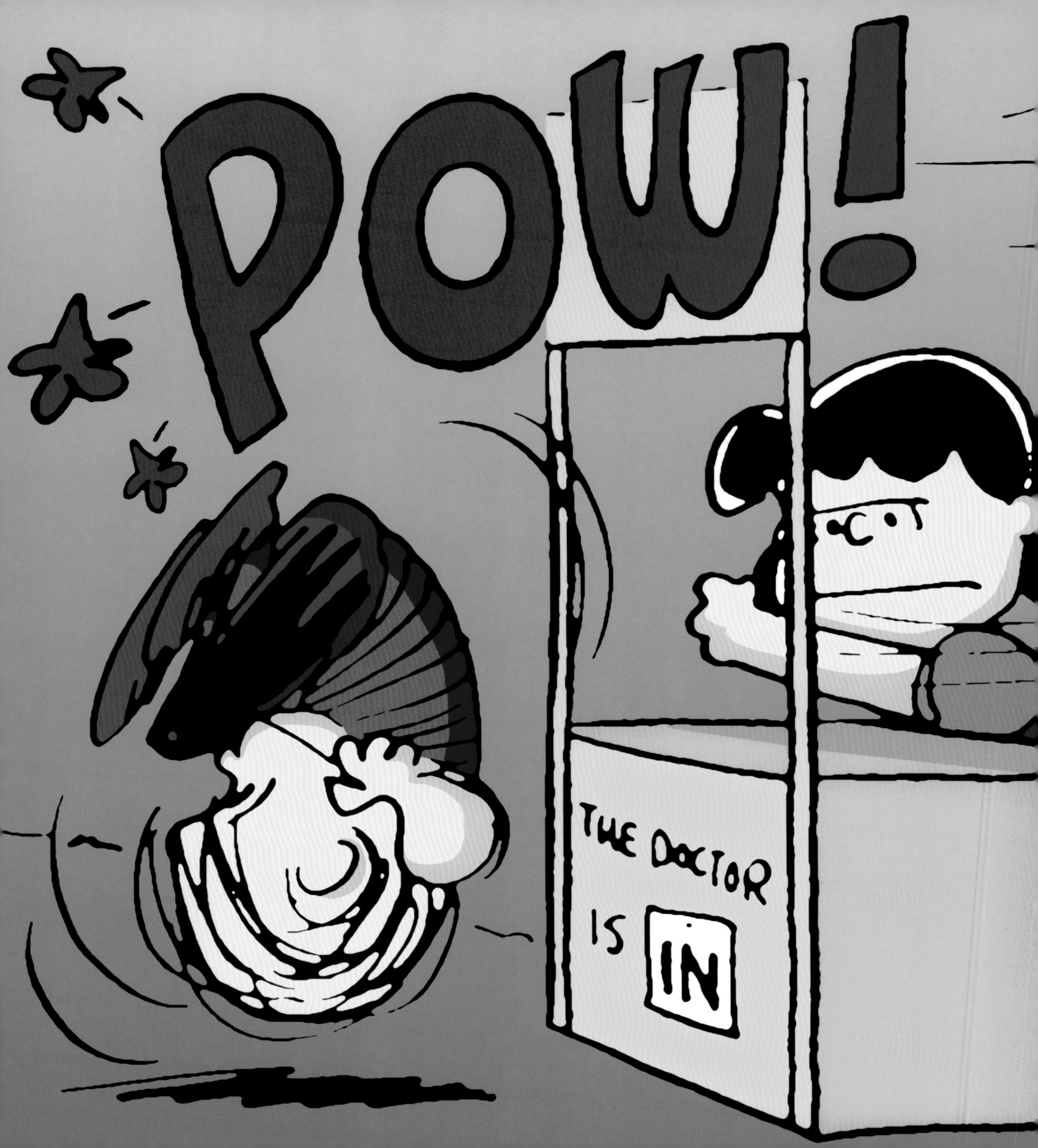
POW!
THE DOCTOR IS IN

PEANUTS
PSYCHIATRIC HELP 5¢
YOU'RE MUCH TOO PASSIVE...
THE DOCTOR IS IN
YOUR PROBLEM, CHARLIE BROWN, IS THAT YOU DON'T REALLY FIGHT WITH LIFE... YOU DON'T DOMINATE IT...
YOU HAVE TO TAKE LIFE BY THE THROAT AND SHAKE IT! YOU HAVE TO KICK IT IN THE STOMACH! YOU HAVE TO PUNCH IT IN THE EYE!
7-29
COULDN'T I JUST YELL AT IT?
THE DOCTOR IS IN
SCHULZ

LUCY'S BLACK-EYE BEAN SOUP

This black bean soup—replete with antioxidants—packs a wallop of flavor!

INGREDIENTS

1 tablespoon olive oil
4 red bell peppers, seeded and diced
3 ribs celery, finely diced
1 onion, finely chopped
½ lb smoked turkey, chicken, or pork sausage, chopped
1 teaspoon ground cumin
1 teaspoon smoked hot paprika
4 cups reduced-sodium chicken broth
2 cans (15 oz each) black beans, drained and rinsed
1 can (14.5 oz) diced tomatoes with juices
2 cups water or additional broth
Salt and freshly ground pepper

Makes 6 to 8 servings

1 In a heavy pot, warm the oil over medium-high heat. Add the peppers, celery, and onion and cook, stirring, until the onion is tender, 5–6 minutes. Add the sausage and cook, stirring, until browned, about 2 minutes. Add the cumin and paprika and stir for 1 minute. Add the broth, beans, and tomatoes and their juices. Bring the soup to a boil, reduce the heat, and simmer to blend the flavors, 20–45 minutes, thinning with water or more broth as desired. Season to taste with salt and pepper.

2 Ladle servings of the soup into insulated containers and close tightly. Let any remaining soup cool, then cover tightly and refrigerate for up to 4 days or freeze individual portions for up to 4 months.

BONK!

PEANUTS
I ALMOST GOT AN "A" ON MY SPELLING TEST
THE ONLY WORD I MISSED WAS "CUCUMBER"
DON'T WORRY ABOUT IT..
THE WAY I SEE IT, A WORD LIKE "CUCUMBER" **DESERVES** TO BE MISSPELLED!
SCHULZ

COOL-AS-A-CUCUMBER SOUP

"Cucumber" may be hard to spell, but it is easy to enjoy in this refreshing soup!

INGREDIENTS

3 English cucumbers, peeled, halved lengthwise, and seeded

1 cup plain whole-milk Greek yogurt

1 tablespoon fresh lemon juice

3 green onions, chopped

3 tablespoons chopped fresh dill

1 clove garlic, minced

1 teaspoon caraway seeds, crushed

1 teaspoon salt

¼ teaspoon ground white pepper

2 tablespoons extra-virgin olive oil

1 cup vegetable broth

Makes 6 servings

1 Coarsely chop 5 of the cucumber halves and transfer to a large bowl. Add the yogurt, lemon juice, green onions, dill, garlic, caraway seeds, salt, and white pepper. Stir to combine, cover, and set aside at room temperature for 1 hour to blend the flavors.

2 Dice the remaining cucumber half. Combine the diced cucumber and olive oil in a small container, close tightly, and refrigerate.

3 Transfer half of the cucumber-yogurt mixture to a blender, add ½ cup of the broth, and purée until smooth. Transfer to an airtight container. Repeat with the remaining cucumber-yogurt mixture and remaining ½ cup broth. Cover the container tightly and refrigerate until well chilled, about 2 hours.

4 Ladle servings of the soup into insulated containers, add the diced cucumber, and close tightly. Cover and refrigerate any remaining soup for up to 4 days.

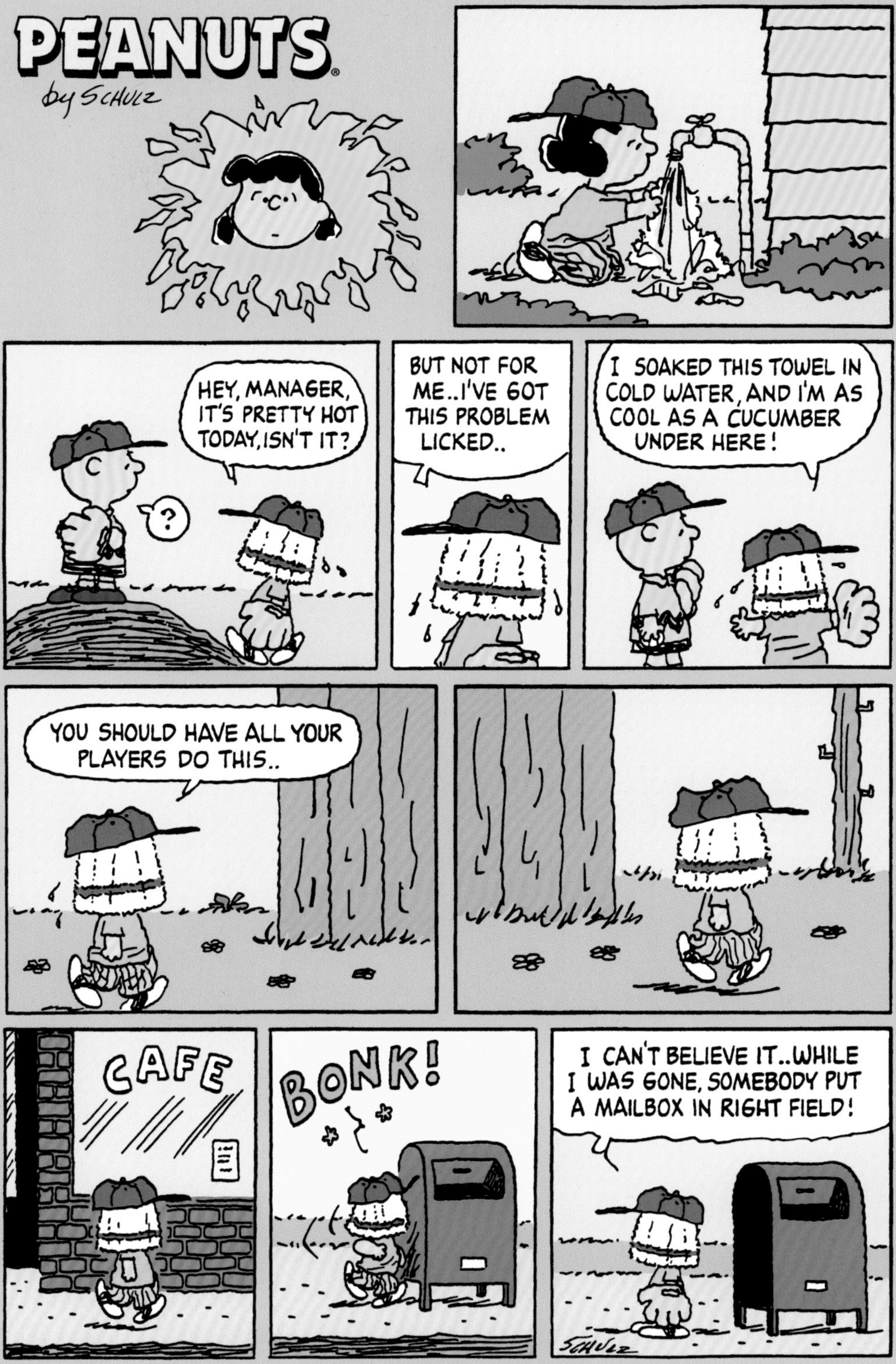

PEANUTS
by SCHULZ
HEY, MANAGER, IT'S PRETTY HOT TODAY, ISN'T IT?
?
BUT NOT FOR ME..I'VE GOT THIS PROBLEM LICKED..
I SOAKED THIS TOWEL IN COLD WATER, AND I'M AS COOL AS A CUCUMBER UNDER HERE!
YOU SHOULD HAVE ALL YOUR PLAYERS DO THIS..
CAFE
BONK!
I CAN'T BELIEVE IT..WHILE I WAS GONE, SOMEBODY PUT A MAILBOX IN RIGHT FIELD!
SCHULZ

PEANUTS
HEY, MR. SACK!
6-25
"MR. SACK"?
REMEMBER HOW I TOLD YOU I COULDN'T FIND MY SHOE?
WELL, I DID LIKE YOU SAID... I LOOKED UNDER MY BUNK AGAIN, AND THERE IT WAS!
YOU'RE A GOOD CAMP PRESIDENT, MR. SACK!
" MR. SACK"?
SCHULZ

MR. SACK'S CAMP CHOWDER

You will have to remove the sack from your head to enjoy the kernels of tastiness in this hearty, creamy corn chowder!

INGREDIENTS

4 ears corn, husks and silk removed
2 slices bacon, cut into ½-inch pieces
5 small boiling potatoes, peeled and diced
2 ribs celery, diced
1 carrot, peeled and diced
½ yellow onion, diced
4 cups reduced-sodium chicken broth
1 cup heavy cream
Salt and freshly ground pepper to taste

Makes 4 to 6 servings

1 Holding 1 ear of corn upright in a bowl with the stem end down, cut straight down between the cob and the kernels, freeing the kernels. Give the ear a quarter turn after each cut. Repeat with the other ears of corn. Discard the cobs.

2 In a stockpot, fry the bacon over medium heat, turning once, until crisp, 8–10 minutes. Add the corn, potatoes, celery, carrot, onion, broth, and cream and stir well. Raise the heat to high and bring to a boil. Reduce the heat to medium-low and simmer until the vegetables are tender, about 20 minutes. Season to taste with salt and pepper.

3 Ladle servings of the soup into insulated containers and close tightly. Let any remaining soup cool, then cover tightly and refrigerate for up to 4 days.

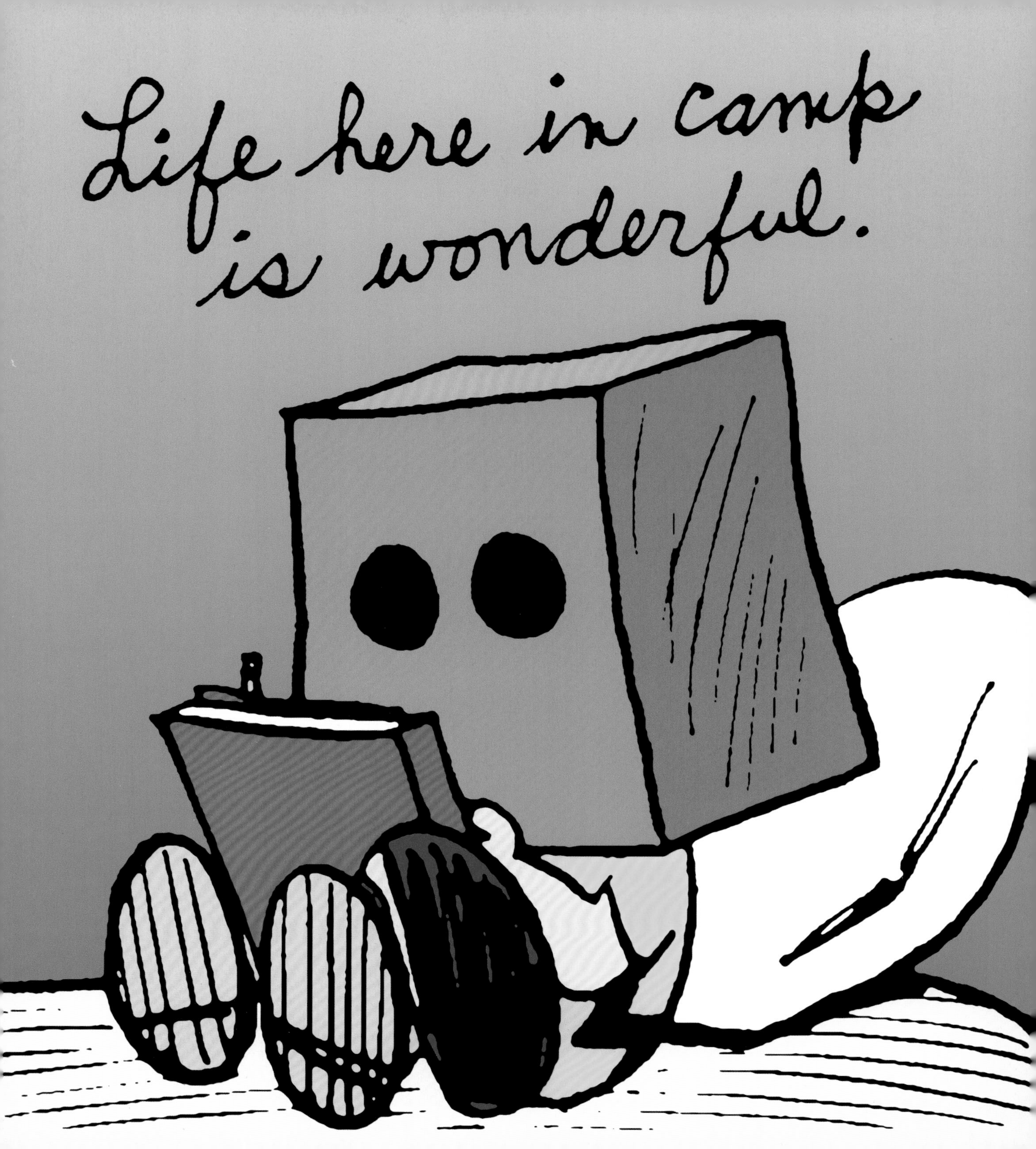
Life here in camp
is wonderful.

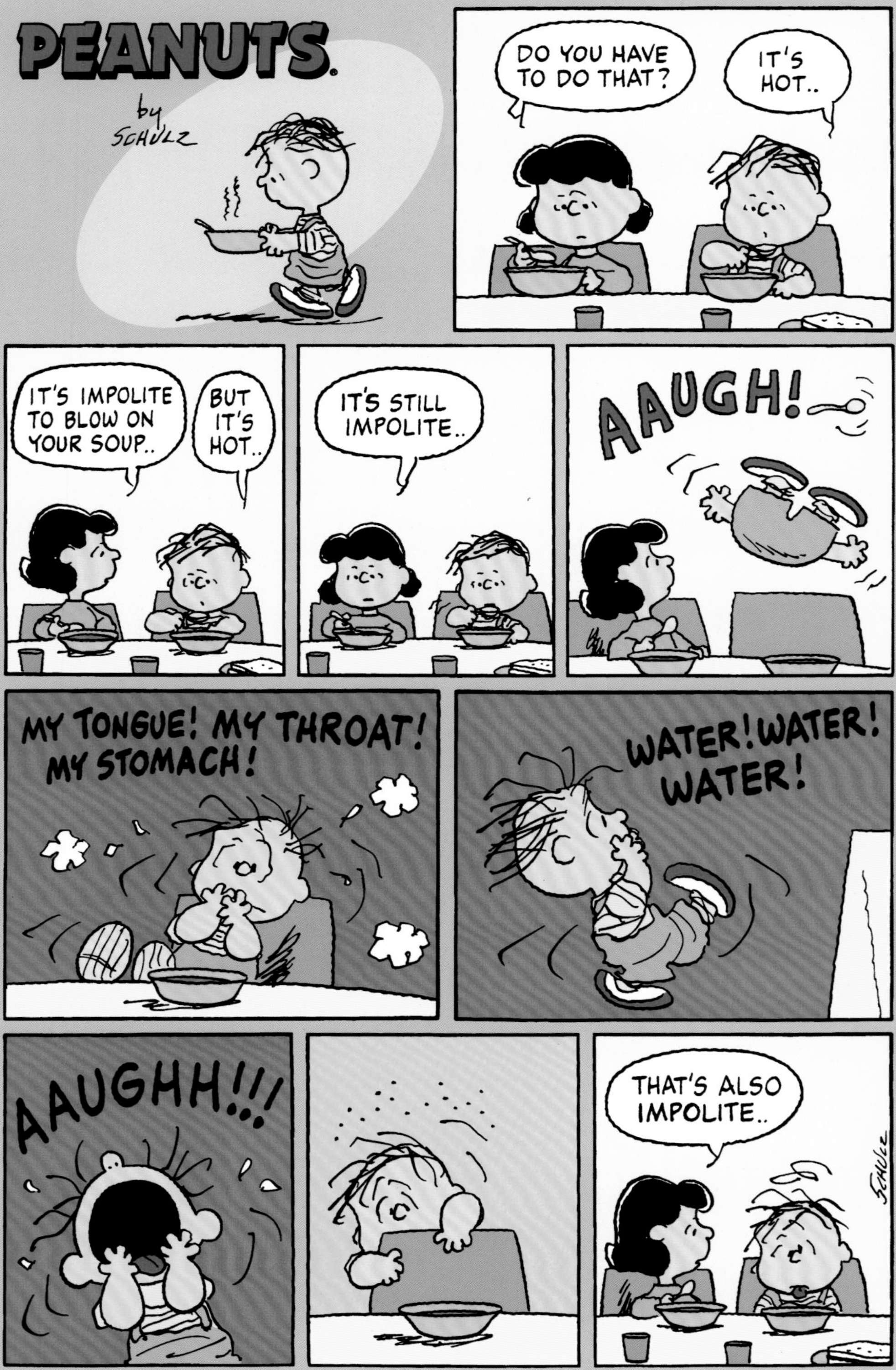
PEANUTS
by SCHULZ
DO YOU HAVE TO DO THAT?
IT'S HOT..
IT'S IMPOLITE TO BLOW ON YOUR SOUP..
BUT IT'S HOT..
IT'S STILL IMPOLITE..
AAUGH!
MY TONGUE! MY THROAT! MY STOMACH!
WATER! WATER! WATER!
AAUGHH!!!
THAT'S ALSO IMPOLITE..
SCHULZ

GUESS WHAT I LEARNED IN SCHOOL TODAY..
WE WERE HAVING LUNCH, AND I LEARNED HOW TO OPEN A BAG OF POTATO CHIPS..
WHAT'S THE CAPITAL OF NORWAY?
WHO KNOWS ?
© 1998 United Feature Syndicate, Inc.
www.snoopy.com
SCHULZ
5-29

RERUN'S HOT & SOUR SOUP

Learn how to cool down with this mildly spicy version of a restaurant favorite.

INGREDIENTS

¾ lb large shrimp, peeled and deveined, and shells reserved
3 lemongrass stalks, white parts only, smashed and cut into 1-inch lengths
5 cups water
5 thin slices galangal
3 fresh or dried makrut lime leaves (optional)
2 tablespoons fish sauce
5 oz white mushrooms, stems trimmed and caps quartered
1 tomato, peeled and cut into thin wedges
¼ small yellow onion, cut lengthwise into thin slivers
4 teaspoons Thai red or green chile paste
2 small red or green chiles such as Thai or serrano, stemmed and quartered lengthwise
¼ cup fresh lime juice, or to taste
¼ cup chopped fresh cilantro

Makes 6 servings

1 In a large saucepan, combine the shrimp shells, lemongrass, and water. Bring to a simmer over medium heat, cover partially, and simmer gently for 15 minutes to blend the flavors. Strain the broth through a fine-mesh sieve into a clean saucepan. Add the galangal, lime leaves (if using), fish sauce, mushrooms, tomato, onion, and chile paste. Add as many of the chile quarters as you like; you may want to start with just a few.

2 Bring the soup to a simmer over medium heat, cover partially, and simmer gently until the mushrooms are barely tender, about 2 minutes. Taste and add more chile quarters if the soup is not spicy enough. Stir in the shrimp and simmer just until they turn pink, about 2 minutes. Remove from the heat. Stir in the lime juice and cilantro. Taste and add more lime juice, if desired.

3 Ladle servings of the soup into insulated containers and close tightly. Let any remaining soup cool, then cover tightly and refrigerate for up to 4 days or freeze individual portions for up to 4 months.

WHAAA!

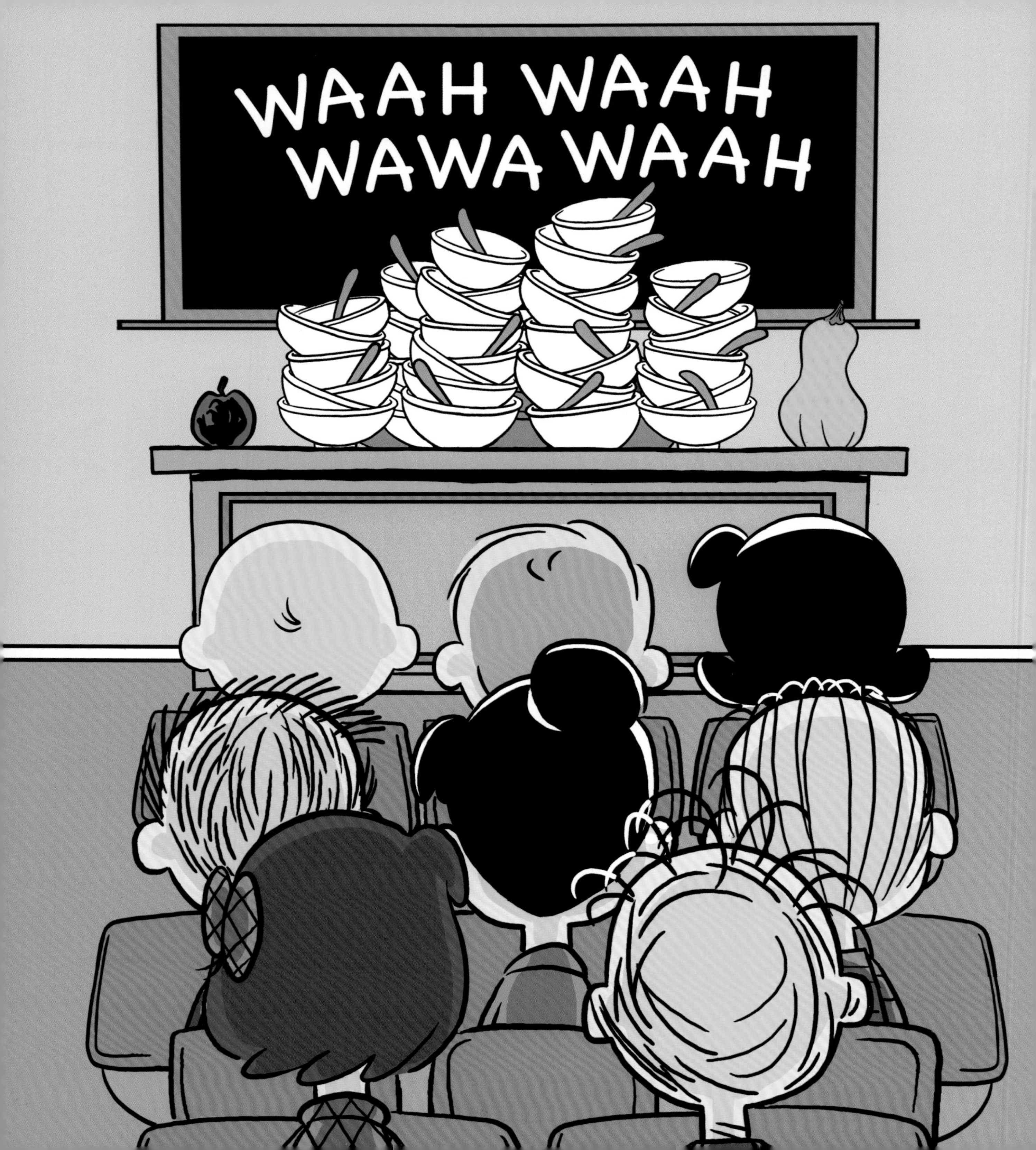
WAAH WAAH
WAWA WAAH

PEANUTS: SO YOU REALLY LIKE YOUR TEACHER, EH, LINUS?

SHE'S A GOOD TEACHER, CHARLIE BROWN...NO, SHE'S MORE THAN JUST A GOOD TEACHER..SHE'S A GREAT HUMAN BEING!

NO, SHE'S MORE THAN A GOOD TEACHER AND A GREAT HUMAN BEING...

MISS OTHMAR IS A GOOD TEACHER, A GREAT HUMAN BEING AND A LIVING DOLL!!

MISS OTHMAR'S APPLE–BUTTERNUT SOUP

Celebrate your favorite teacher by bringing an apple to school—even if it's in a yummy soup mixed with tasty butternut squash.

INGREDIENTS

2 tablespoons unsalted butter

1 small yellow onion, sliced

2 cloves garlic, minced

½ butternut squash (about 2 lb), halved, seeded, peeled, and cut into chunks

2 apples, peeled, cored, and cut into chunks

4 cups vegetable broth or reduced-sodium chicken broth, plus more as needed

Salt and freshly ground pepper

Makes 4 to 6 servings

1 In a large saucepan, melt the butter over medium heat. Add the onion and cook, stirring, until tender, about 8 minutes. Stir in the garlic and cook for 1 minute. Add the squash, apples, and broth, cover, and simmer until the squash is very tender, about 20 minutes. Purée the soup using an immersion blender in the pot. (Alternatively, let the soup cool, then transfer in batches to a regular blender.) Add more broth, if needed, for the desired consistency. Season the soup to taste with salt and pepper.

2 Ladle servings of the soup into insulated containers and close tightly. Let any remaining soup cool, then cover tightly and refrigerate for up to 4 days or freeze individual portions for up to 4 months.

A is for apple

B is for boy

SALADS

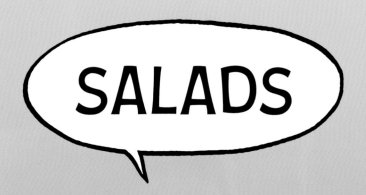

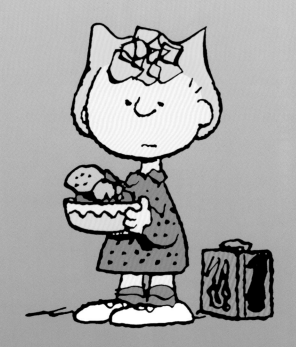

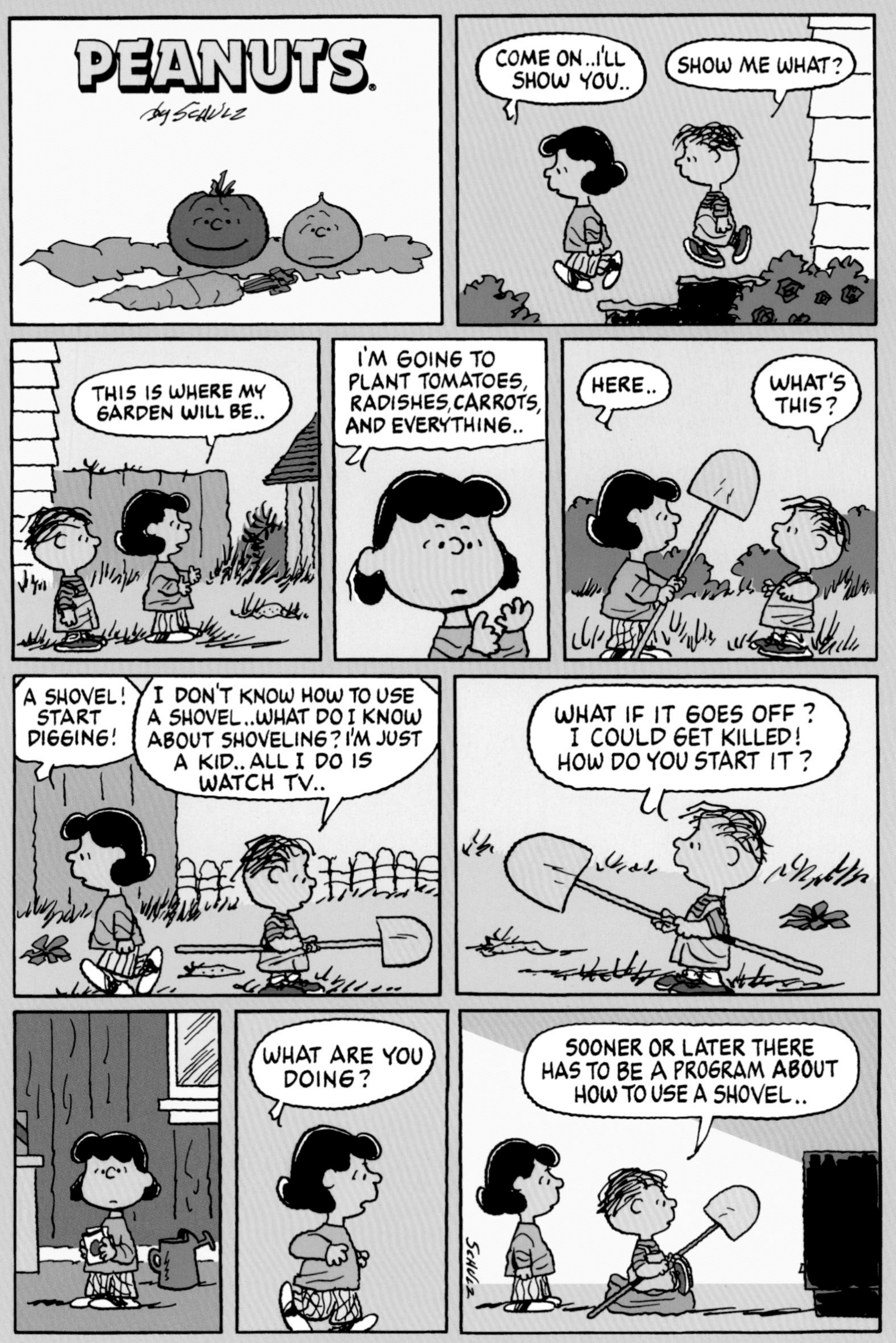
PEANUTS
by SCHULZ
COME ON..I'LL SHOW YOU..
SHOW ME WHAT?
THIS IS WHERE MY GARDEN WILL BE..
I'M GOING TO PLANT TOMATOES, RADISHES, CARROTS, AND EVERYTHING..
HERE..
WHAT'S THIS?
A SHOVEL! START DIGGING!
I DON'T KNOW HOW TO USE A SHOVEL..WHAT DO I KNOW ABOUT SHOVELING? I'M JUST A KID.. ALL I DO IS WATCH TV..
WHAT IF IT GOES OFF? I COULD GET KILLED! HOW DO YOU START IT?
WHAT ARE YOU DOING?
SOONER OR LATER THERE HAS TO BE A PROGRAM ABOUT HOW TO USE A SHOVEL..
SCHULZ

THE WEDDING'S OFF! THE BRIDE RAN AWAY WITH THE GROOM'S BROTHER!
8-26
WHAT ABOUT MY SERMON?
© 1977 United Feature Syndicate, Inc.
WHAT ABOUT THE SALAD I MADE?
I'LL EAT THE SALAD, BUT I WON'T LISTEN TO THE SERMON
SCHULZ

THE VAN PELT SALAD

The Van Pelts throw everything into their take on a Cobb salad—and you can, too!

INGREDIENTS

8 slices bacon
1 head romaine lettuce, leaves separated and torn into bite-size pieces
3 hard-boiled eggs, peeled and cut into bite-size pieces (see page 23)
4 cups (about 1½ lb) chopped cooked turkey or chicken
2 avocados, pitted, peeled, and cubed
2 tomatoes, chopped
5 oz Roquefort or other blue cheese, crumbled (optional)
2 cups chopped stemmed watercress
2 tablespoons minced fresh flat-leaf parsley
2 tablespoons minced fresh chives
¼ cup red wine vinegar
1 teaspoon Worcestershire sauce
½ teaspoon Dijon mustard
1 clove garlic, minced
¼ teaspoon salt
½ teaspoon freshly ground pepper
⅓ cup extra-virgin olive oil

Makes 4 to 6 servings

1 In a frying pan, fry the bacon over medium heat, turning once, until crisp, 8–10 minutes. Transfer to paper towels to drain. Let cool, then crumble.

2 In a large airtight container, arrange the romaine, eggs, turkey, avocados, tomatoes, and 4 oz of the crumbled cheese, if using. Top with the bacon and watercress. Sprinkle the parsley and chives over the salad, then close tightly. Refrigerate until ready to go.

3 In a small airtight container, whisk together the vinegar, Worcestershire sauce, mustard, garlic, salt, and pepper. Using a fork, mash in the remaining 1 oz cheese, if using. Add the oil in a thin stream, whisking until the dressing is smooth. Close tightly. Refrigerate until ready to go, then pack along with the salad in an insulated lunch cooler.

I BRING THE SALAD, THE SANDWICHES, THE PICKLES, THE POTATO CHIPS AND THE ROOT BEER...

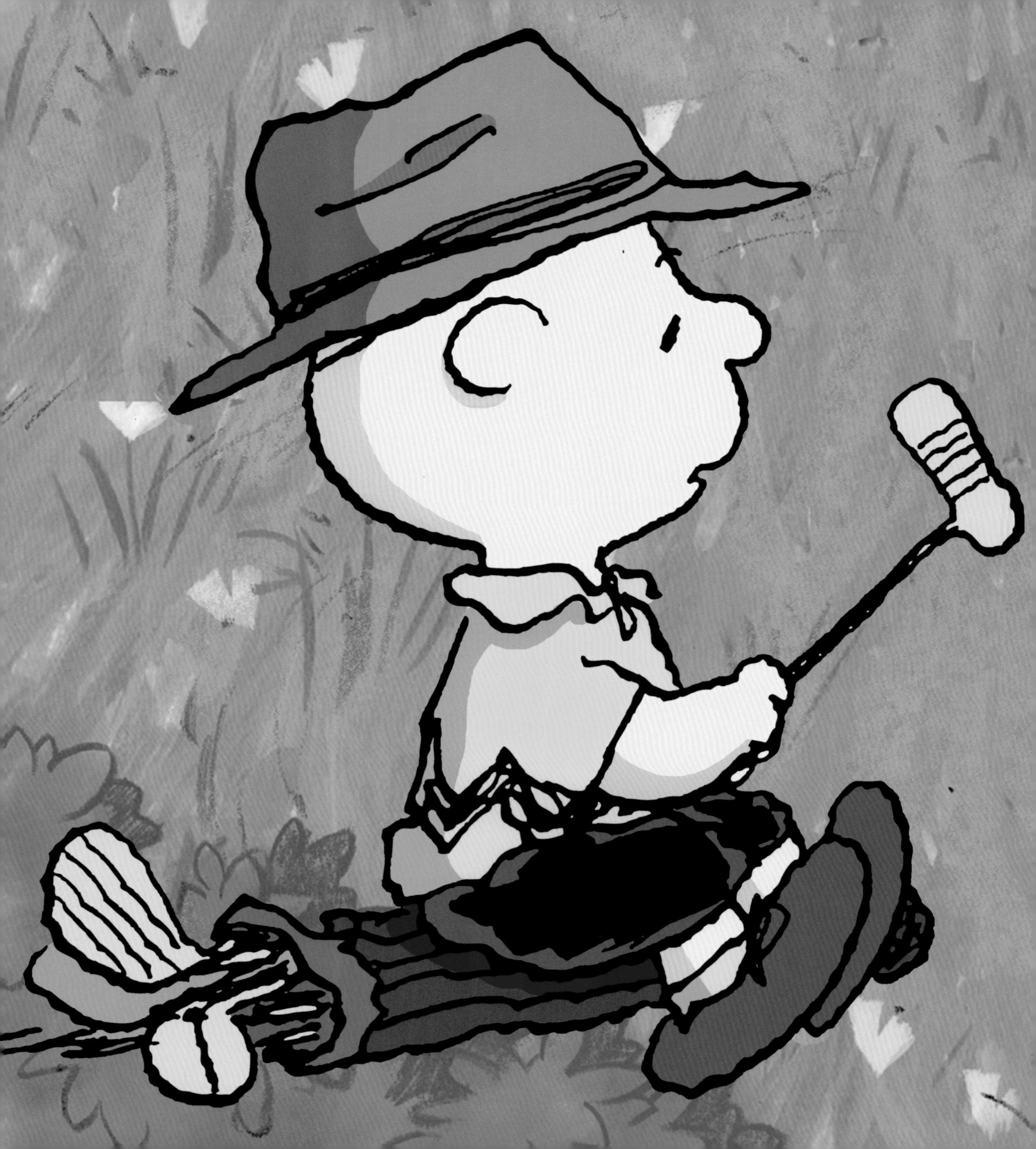

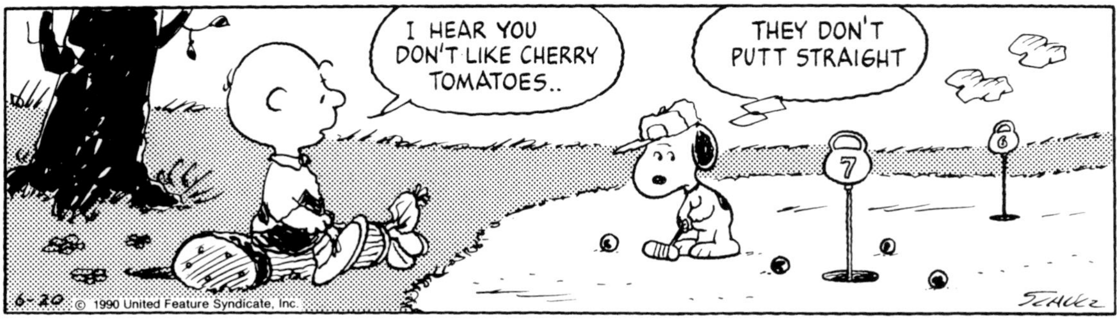
I HEAR YOU DON'T LIKE CHERRY TOMATOES..
THEY DON'T PUTT STRAIGHT
7
6-20 © 1990 United Feature Syndicate, Inc.
SCHULZ

THE CADDYMASTER'S PUTTING GREEN SALAD

Putt little tomatoes into your lunch bag, accompanied by orzo, feta, and black olives. You won't need a caddymaster to help you navigate this course!

INGREDIENTS

Salt and freshly ground pepper
1½ cups orzo
8 cherry tomatoes, quartered
1 cucumber, peeled, seeded, and finely chopped
1 red onion, finely chopped
1 cup crumbled feta cheese
½ cup chopped black olives, drained
¼ cup chopped fresh flat-leaf parsley
1 tablespoon fresh lemon juice, or as needed
½ teaspoon dried oregano
¼ cup extra-virgin olive oil

Makes 6 servings

1 Bring a large pot of lightly salted water to a boil. Add the orzo and cook according to the package directions until just tender. Drain well.

2 In a large airtight container, combine the orzo, tomatoes, cucumber, onion, feta, olives, parsley, lemon juice, oregano, oil, and ½ teaspoon pepper. Toss, then cover and refrigerate for at least 20 minutes. Taste and adjust the seasoning as needed with salt, pepper, and lemon juice. Close tightly. Refrigerate until ready to go, then pack in an insulated lunch cooler.

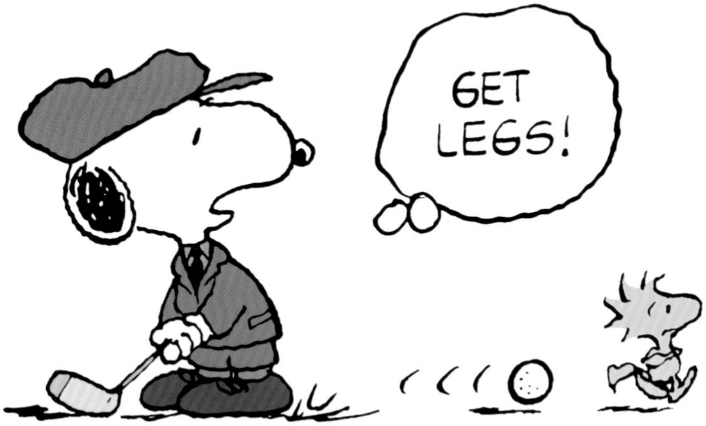
GET LEGS!

PEANUTS
I'VE DECIDED SOMETHING...
IF I EVER GET TO BE A THEOLOGIAN, I'M GOING TO BE WHAT THEY CALL A "THEOLOGIAN IN THE MARKET PLACE"
7-9
SO YOU CAN REACH THE PEOPLE?
Tm. Reg. U.S. Pat. Off.—All rights reserved ©1971 by United Feature Syndicate, Inc.
NO, THAT'S WHERE THE LETTUCE IS!
SCHULZ

CAESAR'S "ROMAINE EMPIRE" SALAD

Friends, Romans, countrymen, lend me your tummies! This Caesar salad will have your chariot racing toward the lunch table.

INGREDIENTS

1 tablespoon mayonnaise
1 clove garlic, chopped
1–3 anchovy fillets, chopped
Juice of 1 lemon
2 teaspoons Dijon mustard
1 teaspoon Worcestershire sauce
¼ cup olive oil
1 teaspoon salt
Freshly ground pepper
1½ cups roughly chopped romaine lettuce
Small wedge Parmesan cheese
¼ cup croutons

Makes 1 serving

1 In a blender, combine the mayonnaise, garlic, anchovy fillets, lemon juice, mustard, Worcestershire sauce, olive oil, salt, and a few grinds of pepper. Blend until the dressing is smooth.

2 Put the lettuce in an airtight container and add the salad dressing as needed. (Transfer any remaining dressing to a jar, close tightly, and store in the refrigerator for up to 5 days.) Cover the container tightly and toss gently until the lettuce is evenly coated with the dressing.

3 Uncover and, using a vegetable peeler, shave thin pieces from the wedge of cheese over the salad. Sprinkle with pepper to taste, then close tightly. Refrigerate until ready to go, then pack along with the croutons in an insulated lunch cooler.

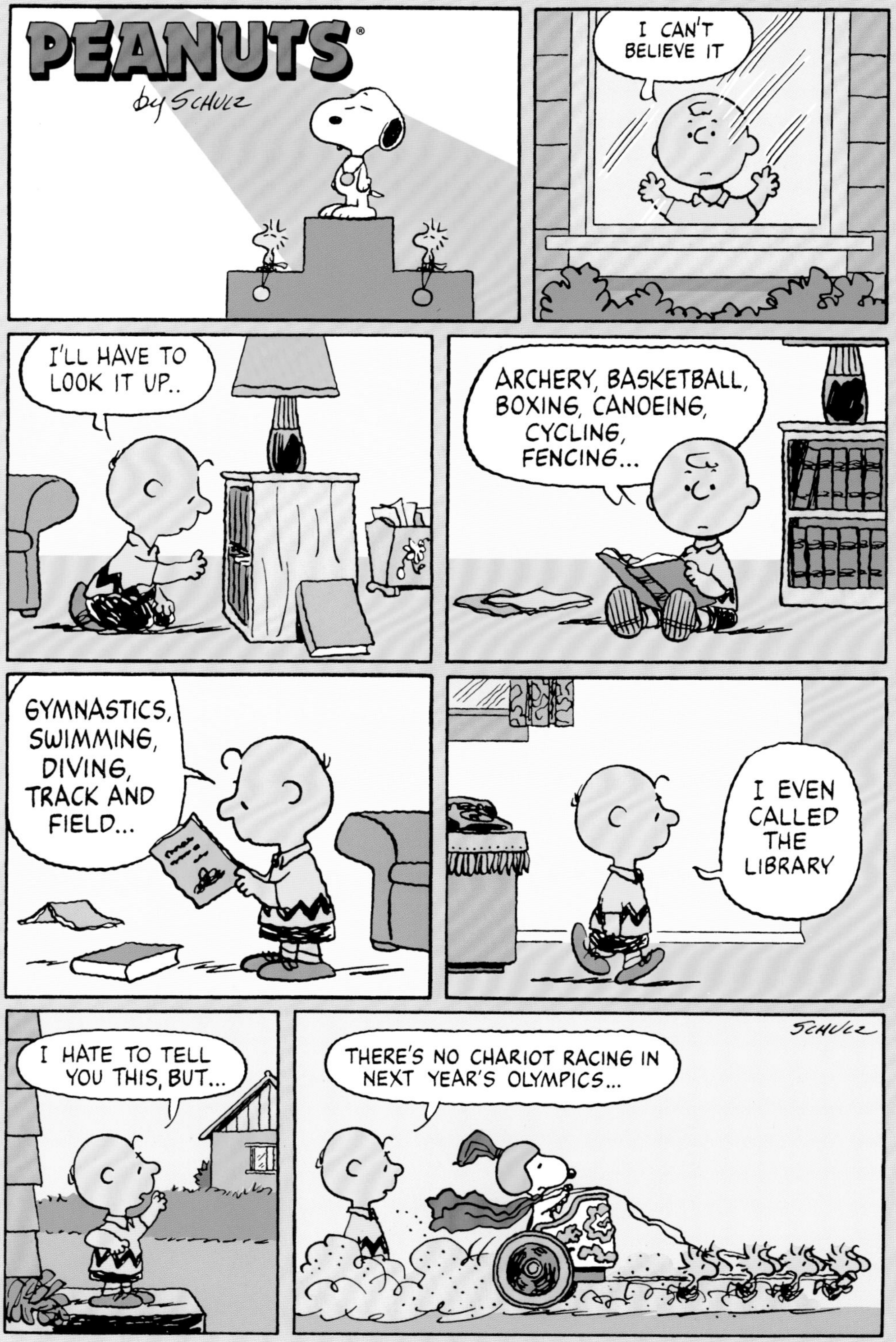
PEANUTS
by SCHULZ
I CAN'T BELIEVE IT
I'LL HAVE TO LOOK IT UP..
ARCHERY, BASKETBALL, BOXING, CANOEING, CYCLING, FENCING...
GYMNASTICS, SWIMMING, DIVING, TRACK AND FIELD...
I EVEN CALLED THE LIBRARY
SCHULZ
I HATE TO TELL YOU THIS, BUT...
THERE'S NO CHARIOT RACING IN NEXT YEAR'S OLYMPICS...

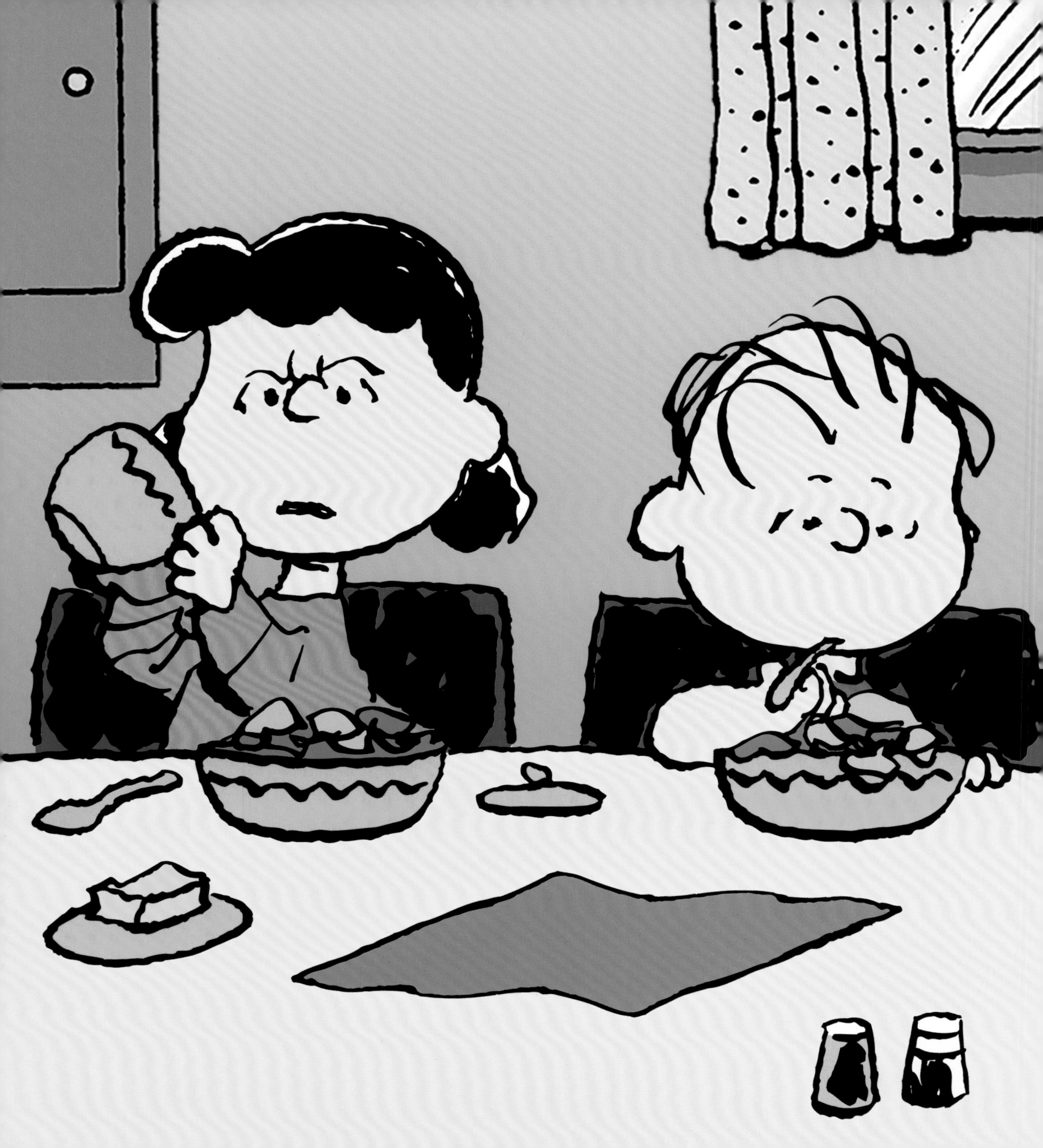

6-8
WHAT ARE YOU PLANTING TODAY?
BRUSSELS SPROUTS
© 1979 United Feature Syndicate, Inc.
IS THIS A GOOD TIME OF YEAR TO PLANT BRUSSELS SPROUTS?
WHO CARES?
BRUSSELS SPROUTS NEVER KNOW WHAT'S GOING ON!
SCHULZ

CAREFREE SHAVED BRUSSELS SPROUTS SALAD

Any time of year is a good time to enjoy nourishing, scrumptious Brussels sprouts. The toasted walnuts give this salad a boost of flavor.

INGREDIENTS

½ cup chopped walnuts
1 lb Brussels sprouts, trimmed
1½ tablespoons walnut oil
1 tablespoon apple cider vinegar
½ teaspoon freshly ground pepper
¼ teaspoon salt
1 cup arugula leaves

Makes 4 servings

1. In a small frying pan, toast the walnuts over medium-low heat, stirring, until starting to brown, about 5 minutes. Let cool.

2. Using a mandoline, thinly shave the Brussels sprouts lengthwise. Put the shaved Brussels sprouts in a bowl and add the walnut oil, vinegar, pepper, and salt and gently mix.

3. Arrange the arugula in an airtight container. Spoon the Brussels sprouts and their juices over the arugula, garnish with the walnuts, and close tightly. Refrigerate until ready to go, then pack in an insulated lunch cooler.

WOULD YOU LIKE A LITTLE COLESLAW WITH YOUR DINNER TONIGHT?
I CHOPPED UP SOME CABBAGE, A FEW CARROTS, A COUPLE OF ONIONS, AND MIXED IN SOME DRESSING...
FORGET IT! I NEVER EAT ANYTHING THAT HAS TO BE EXPLAINED
© 1988 United Feature Syndicate, Inc.
9-24

CHARLIE BROWN'S EASY-TO-EXPLAIN COLESLAW

The uncomplicated tastiness of this crisp, refreshing salad needs no explanation—just dig right in!

INGREDIENTS

FOR THE DRESSING:

1 avocado, halved, pitted, and peeled
2 tablespoons plain whole-milk or low-fat Greek yogurt
2 tablespoons fresh lemon juice
1 teaspoon Dijon mustard
Salt and freshly ground pepper

FOR THE SLAW:

1 package (6 oz) broccoli slaw
½ large Honeycrisp apple, cored and diced
½ cup dried cranberries or currants
½ cup roasted almonds or cashews, chopped

Makes 4 servings

1 To make the dressing, in a bowl, using a fork, mash the avocado until smooth. Add the yogurt, lemon juice, and mustard and stir until well blended. Season to taste with salt and pepper. Transfer to a small airtight container and close tightly.

2 To make the slaw, in a large airtight container, combine the broccoli slaw, apple, and cranberries and toss to mix well. Top with the roasted almonds and close tightly. Refrigerate until ready to go, then pack along with the dressing in an insulated lunch cooler.

YOU KNOW WHAT?
WHAT?

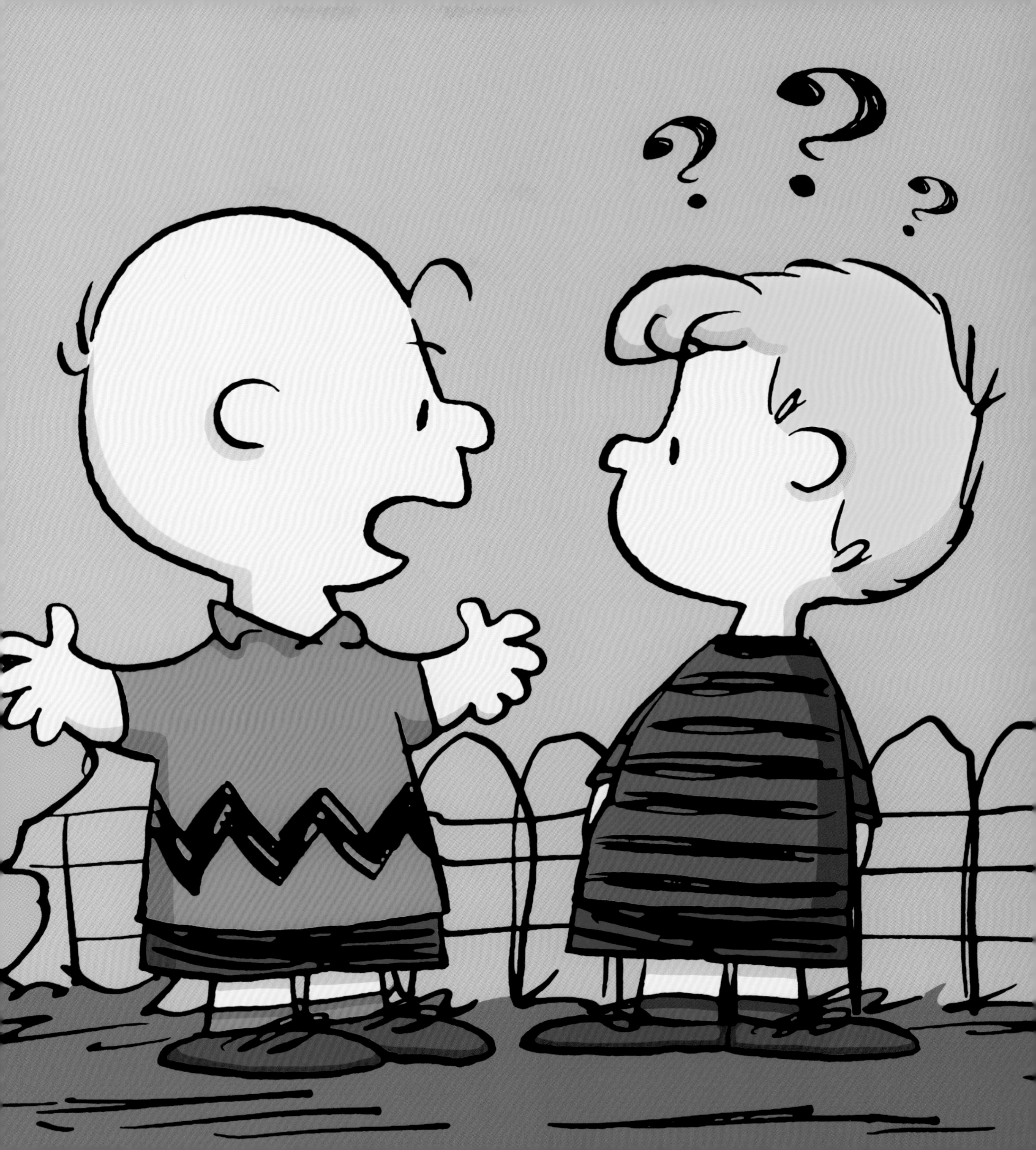

PEANUTS
I DON'T FEEL WELL..
MY HEAD HURTS, AND EVERY TIME I MOVE IT, I GET DIZZY...
I JUST DON'T FEEL WELL...
3-7
SICKEST GUN IN THE WEST!
SCHULZ

DUDE RANCH DIP

Mosey on over to a trough of ranch dressing and dip your favorite veggies in!

INGREDIENTS

¾ cup mayonnaise or Greek yogurt
½ cup buttermilk
¼ cup sour cream
½ bunch fresh flat-leaf parsley, finely chopped
½ bunch fresh chives, finely chopped
Salt and freshly ground pepper
Carrots, celery, bell peppers, or other vegetables, cut into sticks

Makes about 1½ cups

1 In an airtight container, stir together the mayonnaise, buttermilk, and sour cream. Stir in the parsley and chives and season to taste with salt and pepper.

2 Close tightly. Refrigerate until ready to go, then pack along with the crudités in an insulated lunch cooler.

PEANUTS
10-9
THANK YOU FOR THE DANCE!
SCHULZ

LOOSE-LEAF SALAD

Dance with falling spinach leaves fluttering down to mix with olives, eggs, and homemade dressing.

INGREDIENTS

¼ lb sliced bacon
2 apples, cored and chopped
Juice of ½ lemon
1 tablespoon Dijon mustard
1–2 tablespoons balsamic vinegar
Salt and freshly ground pepper
¼ cup extra-virgin olive oil
½ lb spinach or mixed greens
12 black olives, pitted and chopped
2 hard-boiled eggs, cut into wedges (page 23)

Makes 4 servings

1. In a frying pan, fry the bacon over medium heat, turning once, until crisp, 8–10 minutes. Transfer to paper towels to drain. Cut into small pieces.
2. Put the apples in a bowl, sprinkle with the lemon juice, and toss lightly. In a small bowl, stir together the mustard and vinegar and season to taste with salt and pepper. Add the oil and stir vigorously until blended.
3. Arrange the spinach leaves in an airtight container. Add the apples, bacon, olives, and dressing and toss well. Garnish with the egg wedges, if using. Refrigerate until ready to go, then pack in an insulated lunch cooler.

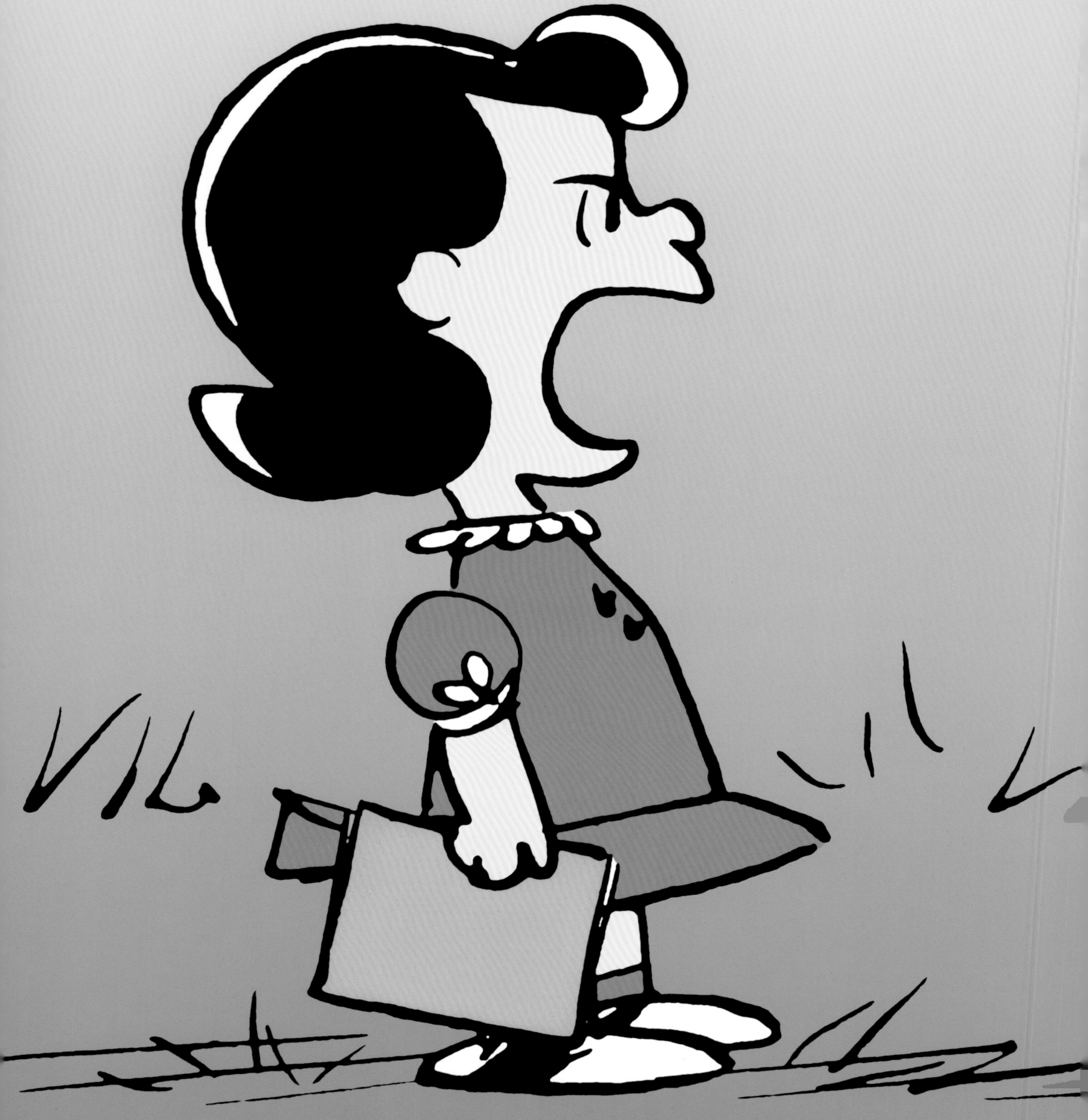

SUMMER GOES BY TOO FAST.. I'LL BET IT RAINS AGAIN TODAY... YESTERDAY WAS TOO HOT..
WE WERE OUT OF COLD CEREAL THIS MORNING.. AND THE STUPID TV WASN'T WORKING AGAIN...
9-30
OUR "FUSSBUDGET IN-RESIDENCE"
© 1987 United Feature Syndicate, Inc.
WHAT'D HE SAY?
SCHULZ

NO-FUSSBUDGET BEAN SALAD

Even the fussiest eaters will have nothing to complain about when they try this tasty green bean salad—a satisfying, healthy, crunchy treat.

INGREDIENTS

Salt and freshly ground pepper
1 lb green beans, trimmed and halved
¼ cup apple cider vinegar
3 tablespoons firmly packed golden brown sugar
3 tablespoons whole-grain mustard
2 tablespoons Dijon mustard
¼ cup chopped fresh chives
1 can (15 oz) chickpeas, drained and rinsed
4 radishes, thinly sliced

Makes 4 servings

1 Bring a large saucepan three-fourths full of salted water to a boil over high heat. Meanwhile, prepare a large bowl of water and ice cubes. Add the green beans to the boiling water and cook until crisp-tender, about 4 minutes. Using a strainer, scoop out the green beans and immerse them in the ice water, then drain and set aside.

2 In a small airtight container, whisk together the vinegar, brown sugar, mustards, and chives until the vinaigrette is well blended. Season to taste with salt and pepper, then close tightly. Refrigerate until ready to go.

3 In a large bowl, toss together the green beans, chickpeas, and radishes. Close tightly. Refrigerate until ready to go, then pack along with the vinaigrette in an insulated lunch cooler.

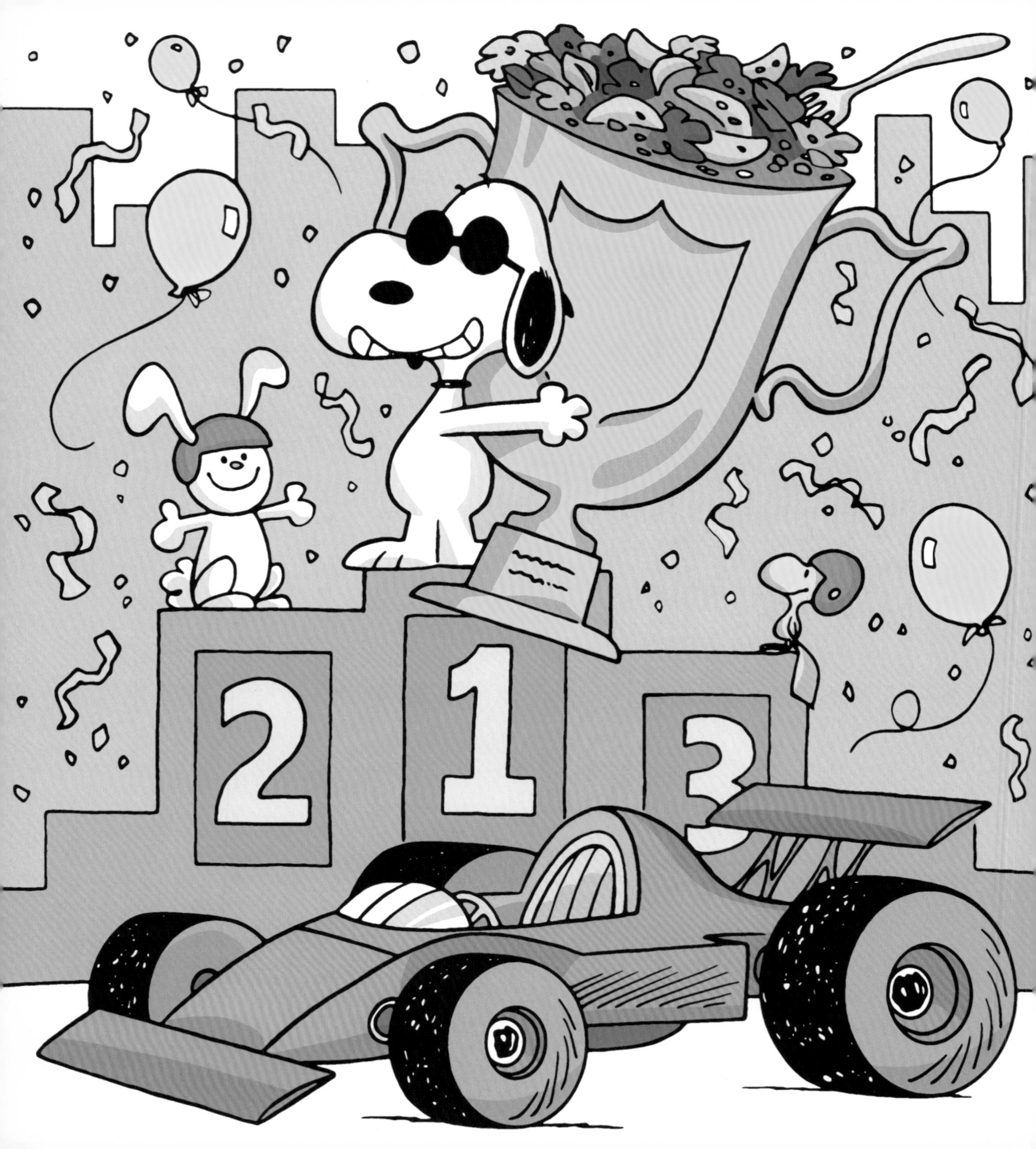
2
1
3

"PEANUTS"
IT MUST BE FRUSTRATING TO BE ABLE TO RUN THAT FAST AND HAVE NO PLACE TO GO...
10-13
SCHULZ

QUICK QUINOA SALAD

You will need to slow down a bit to enjoy the sweet and nutty flavor of this gluten-free salad made with quinoa, an energizing and protein-rich grain.

INGREDIENTS

FOR THE QUINOA SALAD:

1 cup quinoa, rinsed
2 cups water or reduced-sodium chicken broth
½ teaspoon salt
2 cups baby kale
2 small carrots, thinly sliced
¼ cup pomegranate seeds
2 tablespoons fresh mint leaves
2 tablespoons toasted sliced almonds or roasted sunflower seeds
1 tablespoon sesame seeds

FOR THE VINAIGRETTE:

2 tablespoons fresh lemon juice
1 tablespoon white wine vinegar
¼ cup extra-virgin olive oil
Salt and freshly ground pepper

Makes 4 servings

1 To make the quinoa salad, in a small saucepan, combine the quinoa, water, and salt and bring to a boil over high heat. Reduce the heat to low, give the quinoa a stir, cover, and cook, without lifting the lid, until the liquid is absorbed and the quinoa is tender, about 15 minutes. Remove from the heat and let stand, covered, for 5 minutes. Uncover and fluff with a fork, then cover and let cool to room temperature.

2 While the quinoa cools, make the vinaigrette. In a small airtight container, combine the lemon juice, vinegar, and oil. Cover and shake until evenly blended. Season to taste with salt and pepper, then close tightly. Refrigerate until ready to go.

3 In a large airtight container, combine the quinoa, kale, carrots, pomegranate seeds, mint, almonds, and sesame seeds and toss to mix evenly. Close tightly. Refrigerate until ready to go, then pack along with the vinaigrette in an insulated lunch cooler.

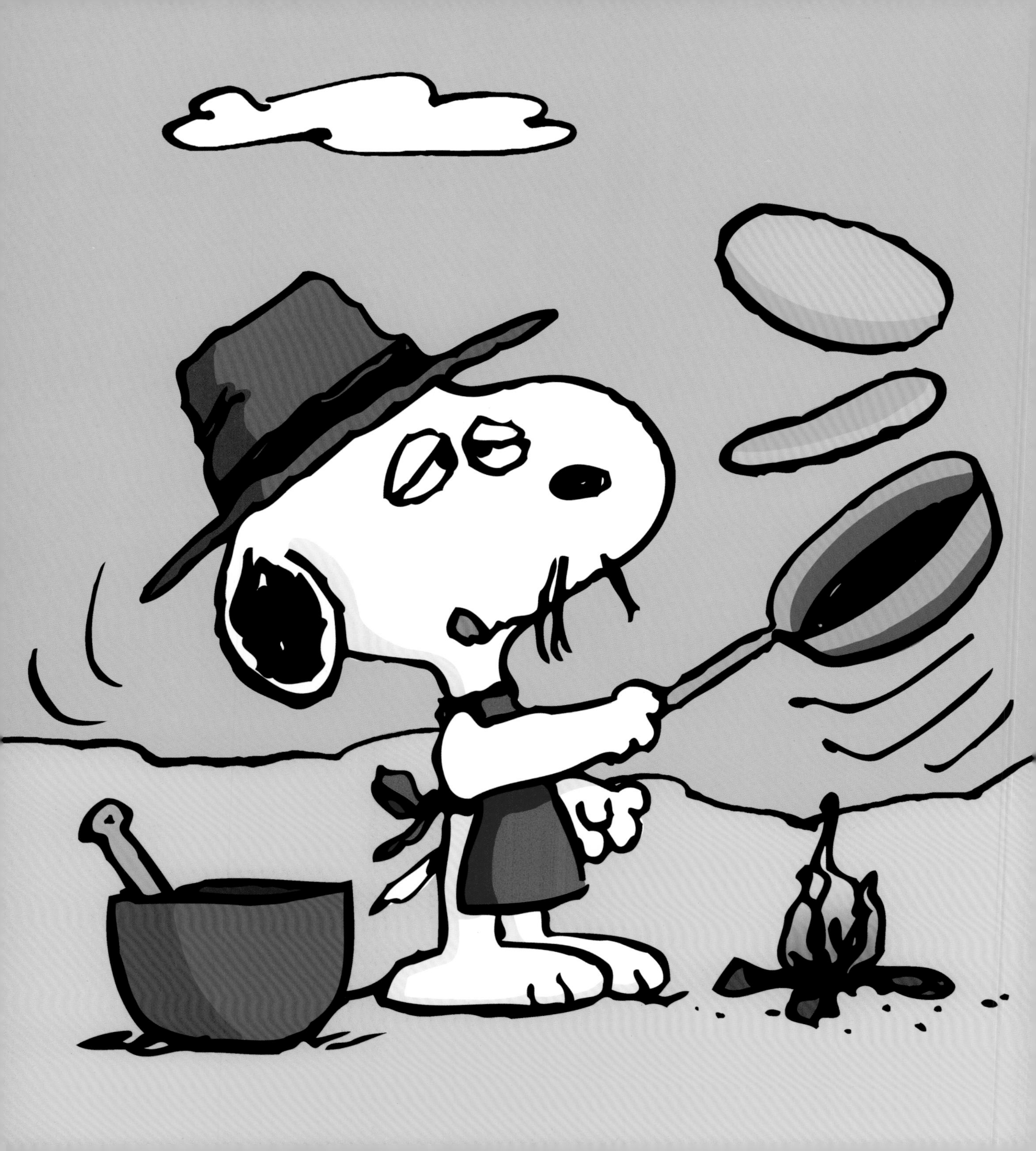

WHEN YOU LIVE ALONE IN THE DESERT, YOU HAVE TO MAKE YOUR OWN PLEASURES...
© 1984 United Feature Syndicate, Inc.
GARÇON..
1-20
A MENU, PLEASE
SCHULZ

SPIKE'S NORTH-OF-THE-BORDER TACO SALAD

Bring south-of-the-border flavors to your north-of-the-border lunch box.

INGREDIENTS

- 2 tablespoons Fresh Tomato Salsa (page 118)
- 1 tablespoon sour cream
- ¼ cup shredded Monterey Jack cheese
- ⅓ cup crumbled tortilla chips
- 1½ cups shredded lettuce
- ¼ cup chopped tomato
- ¼ cup canned black, kidney, or pinto beans, drained and rinsed
- 2 tablespoons sliced black olives

Makes 1 to 2 servings

1. In a small airtight container, stir together the salsa and sour cream to make a dressing. In another small airtight container, combine the cheese and crumbled tortilla chips.

2. In a large airtight container, combine the lettuce, tomato, beans, and olives and toss to combine the ingredients. Close tightly. Refrigerate until ready to go, then pack along with the salsa dressing and cheesy chip topping in an insulated lunch cooler.

SMACK

SNACKS

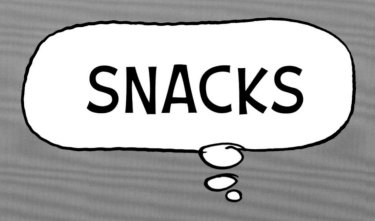

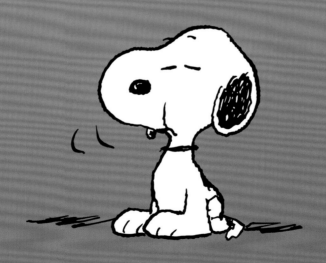

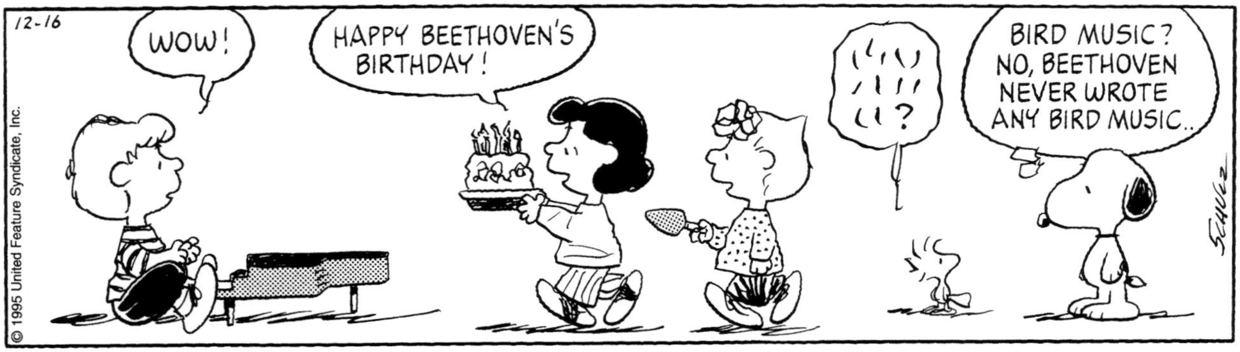
12-16
© 1995 United Feature Syndicate, Inc.
WOW!
HAPPY BEETHOVEN'S BIRTHDAY!
BIRD MUSIC? NO, BEETHOVEN NEVER WROTE ANY BIRD MUSIC..
SCHULZ

BEETHOVEN'S BIRTHDAY PARTY MIX

The symphony of flavors in this crispy snack—salty, savory, and slightly spicy—will make it center stage in your lunch bag or even at a party.

INGREDIENTS

2 tablespoons unsalted butter
1 tablespoons Worcestershire sauce
1 teaspoon sugar
1 teaspoon seasoned salt such as Lawry's
½ teaspoon onion powder
¼ teaspoon garlic powder
2 cups Chex cereal, in any combination of wheat, rice, and/or corn
¼ cup mixed nuts
¼ cup bite-size pretzels
¼ cup bite-size Cheddar crackers

Makes about 6 servings

1 Preheat the oven to 250°F. Put the butter in a shallow baking dish and set in the oven until melted. Stir in the Worcestershire sauce, sugar, seasoned salt, onion powder, and garlic powder until blended. Add the cereal, nuts, pretzels, and crackers and toss gently but thoroughly to coat with the seasoned butter.

2 Spread out the cereal mixture evenly in the dish and bake for 45 minutes, stirring every 10 minutes. Let cool. Pack in an airtight container, close tightly, and store for up to 2 weeks.

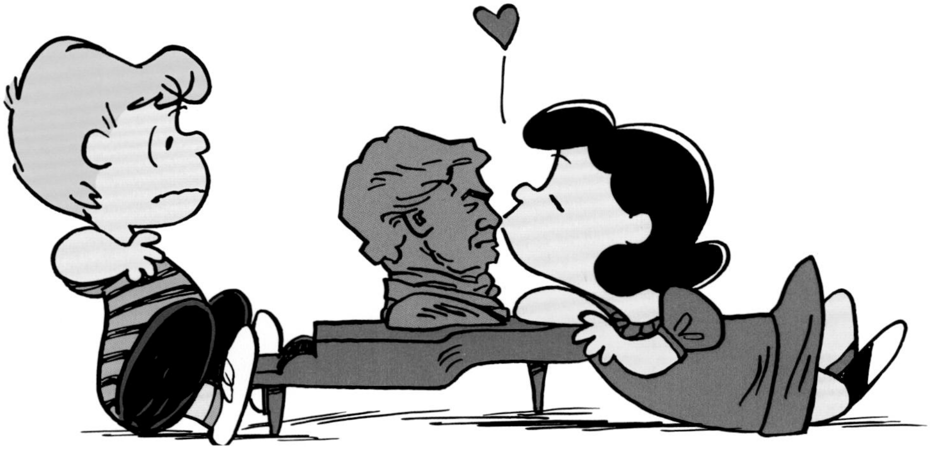

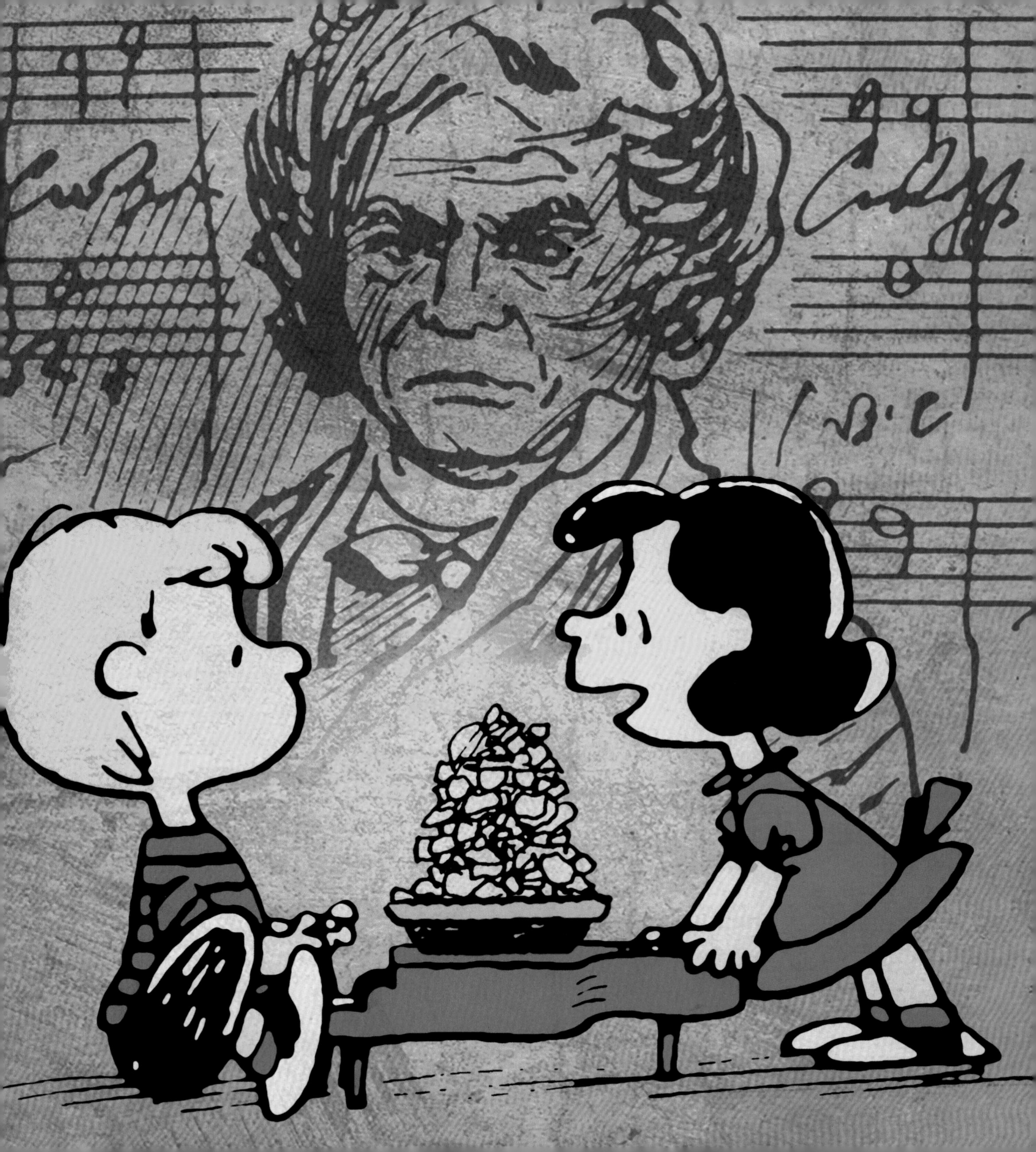

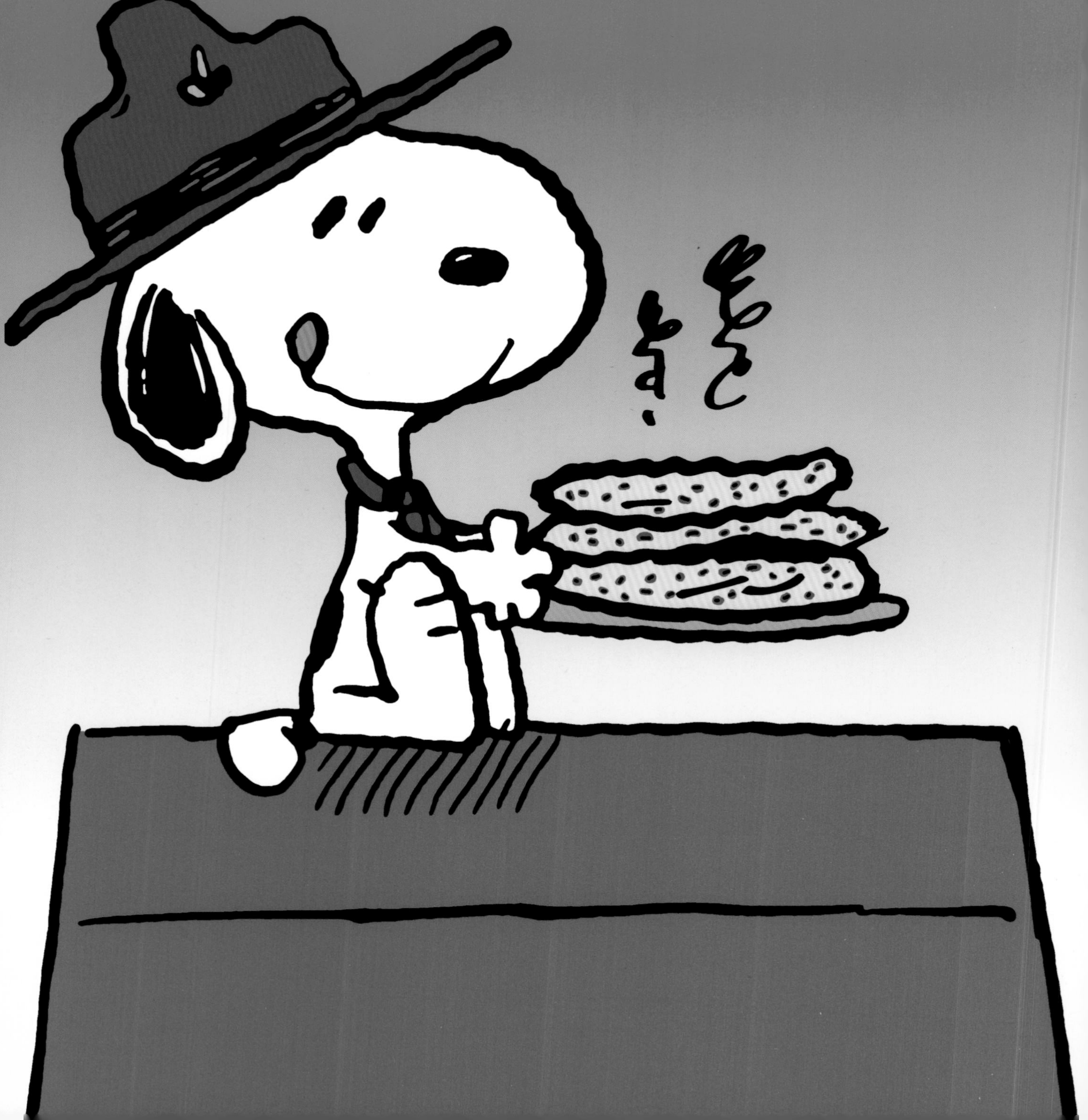

..MIX TOGETHER AND ADD SLOWLY ONE CUP SELF RISING FLOUR TO MIX...
DO NOT MAKE BATTER TOO SOFT..IT MUST DROP FROM A TABLESPOON INTO HOT FAT ABOUT ONE INCH DEEP IN FRYING PAN...
© 1979 United Feature Syndicate, Inc.
11-26
HOW CAN YOU THINK ZUCCHINI FRITTERS AND STILL GET DOG FOOD?

DOGHOUSE ZUCCHINI FRITTERS

No need to fritter away the time dreaming of the ideal snack – these wholesome fritters will top the list of your doghouse treats!

INGREDIENTS

1 zucchini
½ teaspoon salt
1 large egg, beaten
3 tablespoons grated Parmesan cheese
1 clove garlic, minced
1 green onion, finely chopped
¼ teaspoon dried parsley
Freshly ground pepper to taste
¼ cup all-purpose flour
¼ teaspoon baking powder
2 tablespoons olive oil
Greek yogurt for dipping (optional)

Makes about 5 fritters

1 Grate the zucchini using a box grater. In a bowl, toss the zucchini and salt, and let sit for 10 minutes. Wrap the shredded zucchini in cheesecloth and squeeze to drain the excess liquid.

2 In a large bowl, combine the zucchini, egg, cheese, garlic, onion, parsley, and pepper. Sprinkle the flour and baking powder evenly over the mixture and stir until just incorporated.

3 Heat the olive oil over medium-high heat. Spoon about a tablespoon of the zucchini mixture into the pan. Use the back of a spatula to flatten them, and cook until deep golden brown, about 2–3 minutes. Flip and cook the other side until golden brown, about 2–3 minutes more, then transfer to a plate. Repeat with remaining zucchini mixture.

4 Let the fritters cool for 5 minutes, then transfer to an airtight container and close tightly. Refrigerate until ready to go, then pack along with the Greek yogurt, if using, in an insulated lunch cooler.

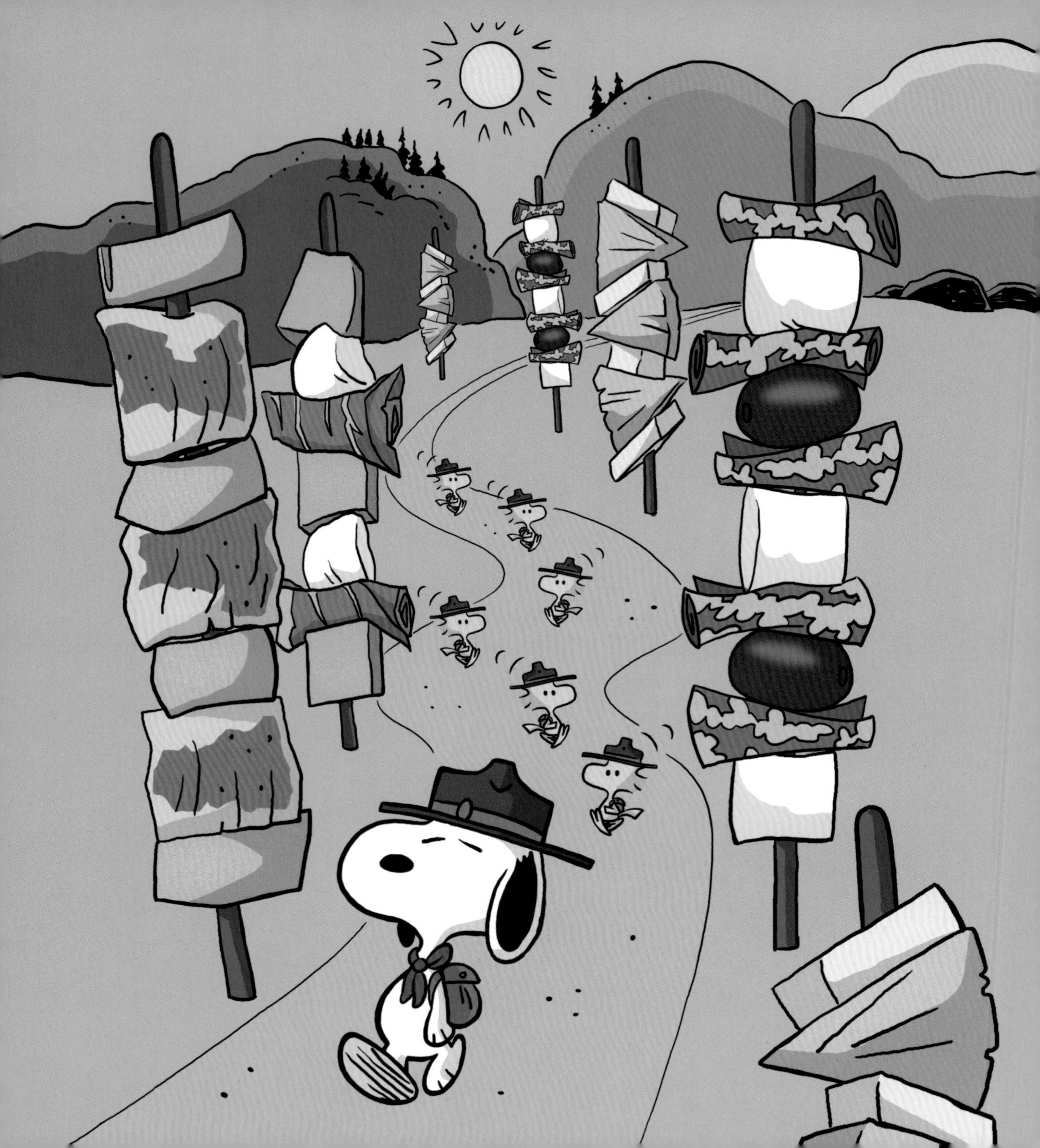

ALL RIGHT, TROOPS.. TODAY I'M GOING TO GIVE YOU A LESSON IN SURVIVAL..
LET'S SAY WE'RE LOST IN THE WOODS... WHAT DO WE DO ABOUT FOOD?
2-8
SHOOT A MOOSE?
SCHULZ
©1978 United Feature Syndicate, Inc.

EAGLE CAMP KEBABS

There are few things more fun than a snack on a stick . . . except perhaps winding your way through all the yummy flavor combinations!

INGREDIENTS

PIZZA KEBABS:

6 grape or cherry tomatoes
6 basil leaves, torn into bite-size pieces
6 fresh mozzarella balls
Salt and pepper to taste

CHICKEN BBQ KEBABS:

2 breasts grilled chicken, cubed
1 bell pepper, seeded and diced
BBQ sauce, for dipping

HAWAIIAN KEBABS:

¼ lb thickly sliced ham, cubed
⅓ cup pineapple chunks

CHARCUTERIE KEBABS:

6 slices salami, rolled up
1 stick string cheese or other cheese, cubed
6 pitted black or green olives

Makes 2 kebabs per recipe

1. Have ready short wooden skewers or toothpicks. Working with one skewer at a time, alternately thread your choice of ingredients onto each skewer.

2. Arrange the kebabs in an airtight container, placing any sauces in a separate container, and close tightly. Refrigerate until ready to go, then pack in an insulated lunch cooler.

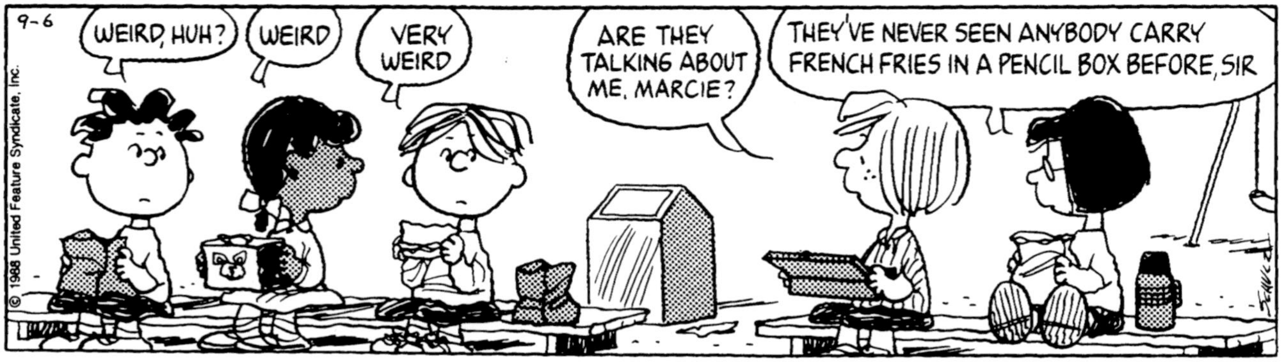

WEIRD, HUH?
WEIRD
VERY WEIRD
ARE THEY TALKING ABOUT ME, MARCIE?
THEY'VE NEVER SEEN ANYBODY CARRY FRENCH FRIES IN A PENCIL BOX BEFORE, SIR
© 1988 United Feature Syndicate, Inc.

PEPPERMINT PATTY'S PENCIL BOX FRIES

There is nothing weird about having French fries with homemade ketchup for a snack. Just make sure your pencil box is big enough to hold them all!

INGREDIENTS

- 1 lb sweet potatoes
- 1 tablespoon olive oil
- 1/8 teaspoon coarse sea salt
- 1 tablespoon chopped fresh flat-leaf parsley
- 1 clove garlic, minced
- Homemade Ketchup (page 118)

Makes about 3 servings

1 Preheat the oven to 450°F. Rinse and dry the sweet potatoes, but do not peel them. Cut the sweet potatoes lengthwise into slices ½ inch thick, then cut each slice into long batons about ¼ inch wide. Arrange in a single layer on a rimmed baking sheet and toss with the olive oil and salt. Roast, stirring halfway through the baking time, until tender and browned on the edges, 20–25 minutes.

2 Remove the fries from the oven. In a large airtight container, stir together the parsley and garlic. Add the warm fries to the container and mix gently to coat. Season to taste with more salt, if needed. Close tightly. Refrigerate until ready to go, then pack along with the ketchup in an insulated lunch cooler.

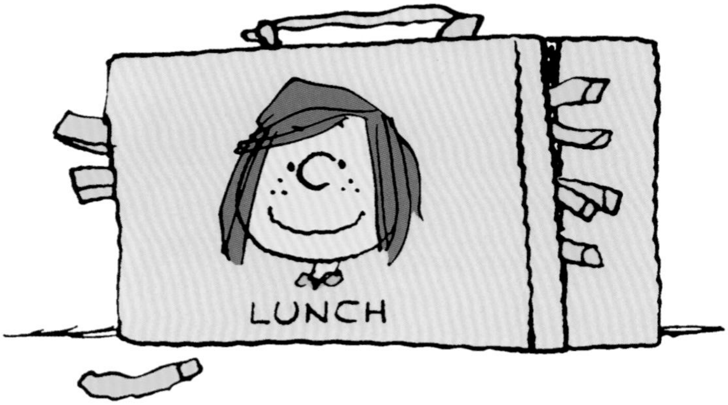

LUNCH

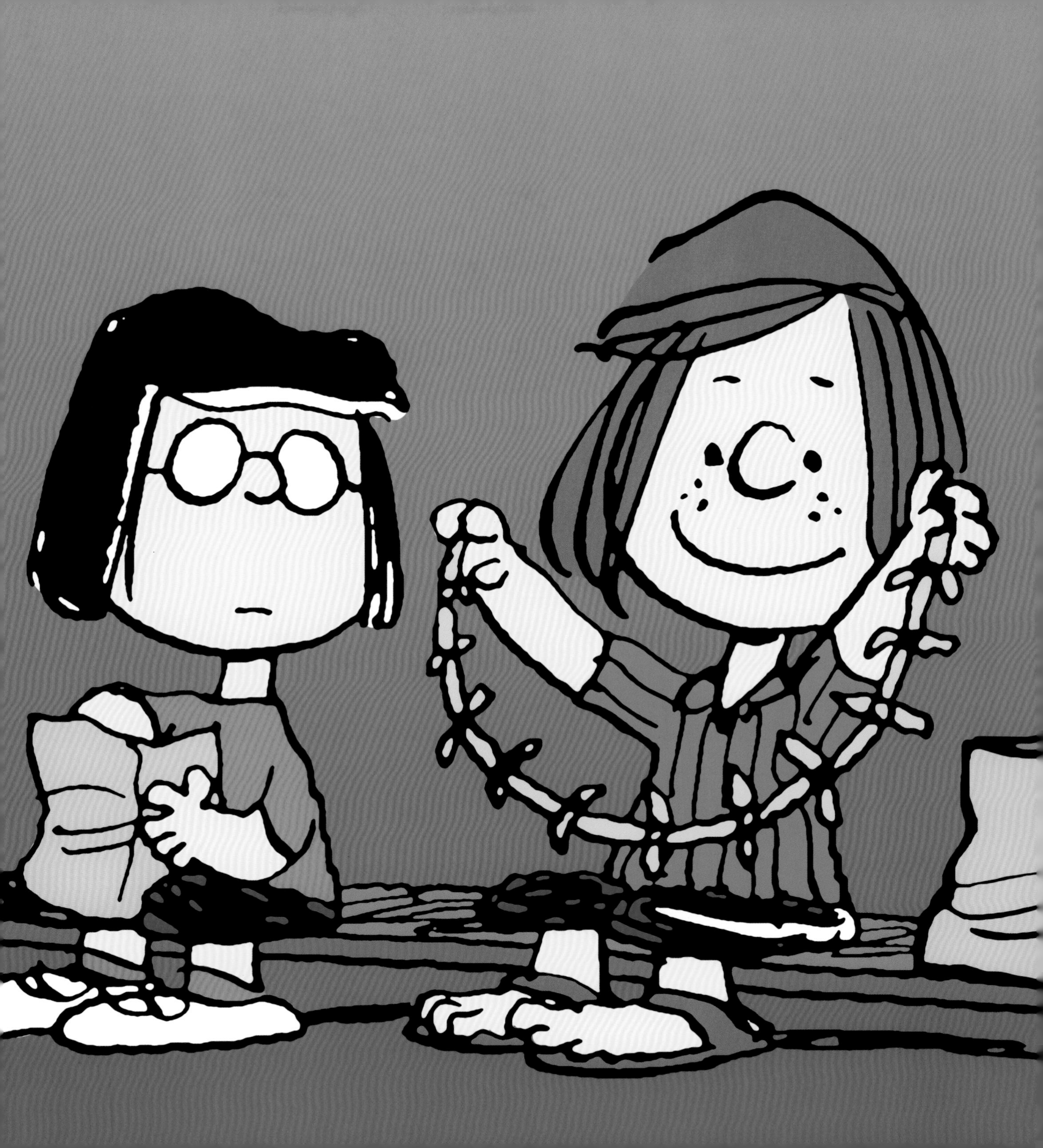

PEANUTS
OH, NO, YOU DON'T!
YOU GET FED **AFTER** THE GAME, NOT **BEFORE**!
Tm. Reg. U.S. Pat. Off.—All rights reserved © 1971 by United Feature Syndicate, Inc.
I HATE THESE SALARY DISPUTES
SCHULZ

OUT-OF-THE-PARK CRACKERS

These cheesy slice-and-bake cracker rounds are an ideal bite for the outfield. Just don't store them in your glove!

INGREDIENTS

- 2 cups shredded Comté or Gruyère cheese
- ½ cup grated Parmesan cheese
- 6 tablespoons unsalted butter
- 1 cup all-purpose flour
- Pinch of cayenne pepper
- 2–3 tablespoons chopped fresh thyme
- Coarse sea salt

Makes about 2 dozen crackers

1 In a food processor, combine the cheeses, butter, flour, and cayenne and process until well combined and crumbly, 40–60 seconds. Transfer the mixture to a sheet of plastic wrap and shape into a log about 2 inches in diameter and 6–7 inches long. Roll up the log in the plastic wrap, patting it to form a smooth, even cylinder. Refrigerate for at least 1 hour or up to overnight.

2 Preheat the oven to 350°F. Unwrap the dough and slice into rounds about ¼ inch thick. Arrange on 2 ungreased rimmed baking sheets, preferably nonstick, spacing them about 2 inches apart. Sprinkle the rounds evenly with the thyme and top each with a pinch of salt.

3 Bake the crackers, 1 sheet at a time, rotating the pan front to back halfway through the baking time, until light golden brown, 10–15 minutes. For crispier crackers, bake for up to 3 minutes longer, watching carefully to avoid overbrowning. Let cool in the pan on a wire rack, then transfer to an airtight container, close tightly, and store for up to 5 days.

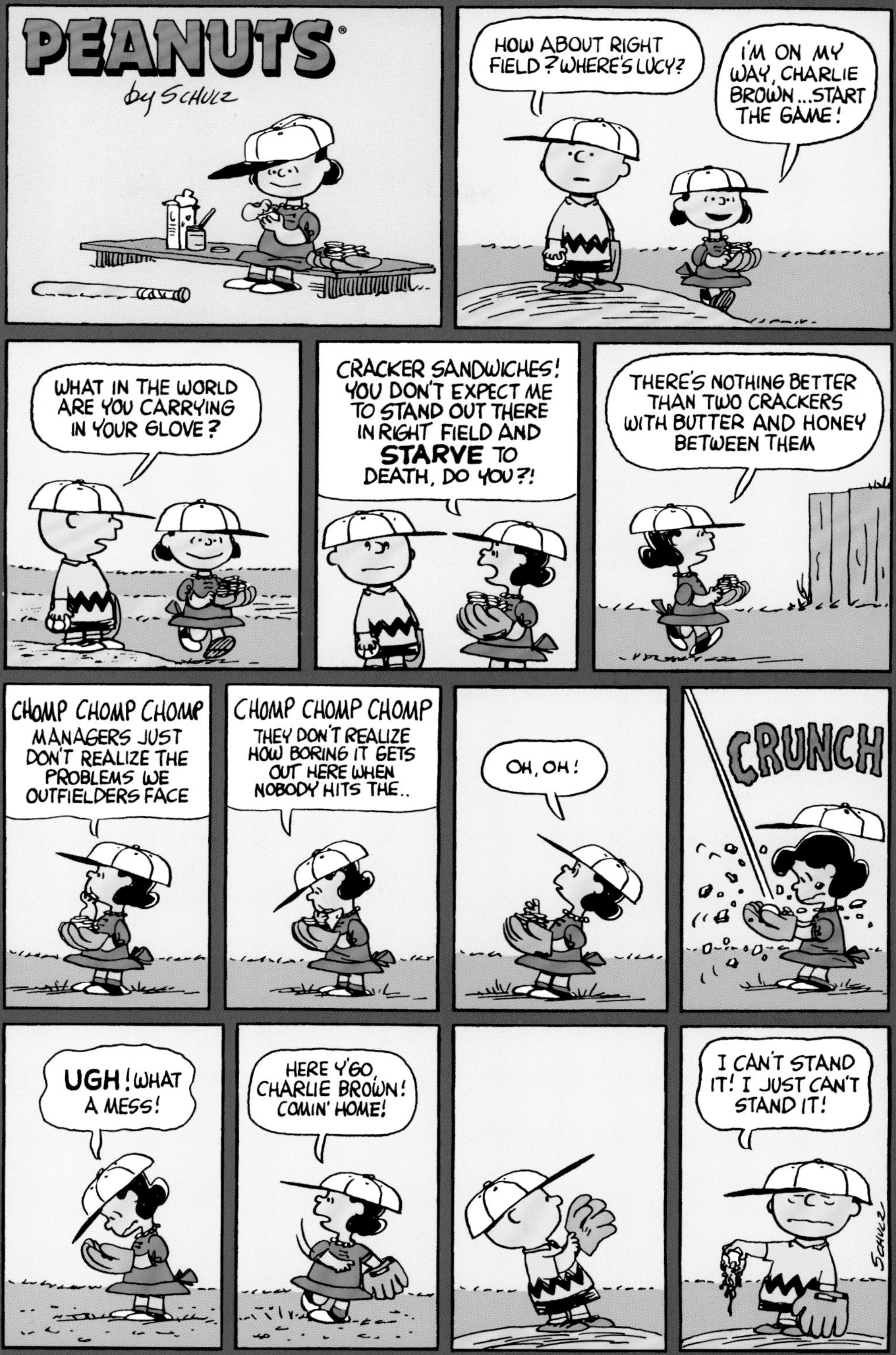
PEANUTS
by SCHULZ
HOW ABOUT RIGHT FIELD? WHERE'S LUCY?
I'M ON MY WAY, CHARLIE BROWN...START THE GAME!
WHAT IN THE WORLD ARE YOU CARRYING IN YOUR GLOVE?
CRACKER SANDWICHES! YOU DON'T EXPECT ME TO STAND OUT THERE IN RIGHT FIELD AND STARVE TO DEATH, DO YOU?!
THERE'S NOTHING BETTER THAN TWO CRACKERS WITH BUTTER AND HONEY BETWEEN THEM
CHOMP CHOMP CHOMP
MANAGERS JUST DON'T REALIZE THE PROBLEMS WE OUTFIELDERS FACE
CHOMP CHOMP CHOMP
THEY DON'T REALIZE HOW BORING IT GETS OUT HERE WHEN NOBODY HITS THE..
OH, OH!
CRUNCH
UGH! WHAT A MESS!
HERE Y'GO, CHARLIE BROWN! COMIN' HOME!
I CAN'T STAND IT! I JUST CAN'T STAND IT!
SCHULZ

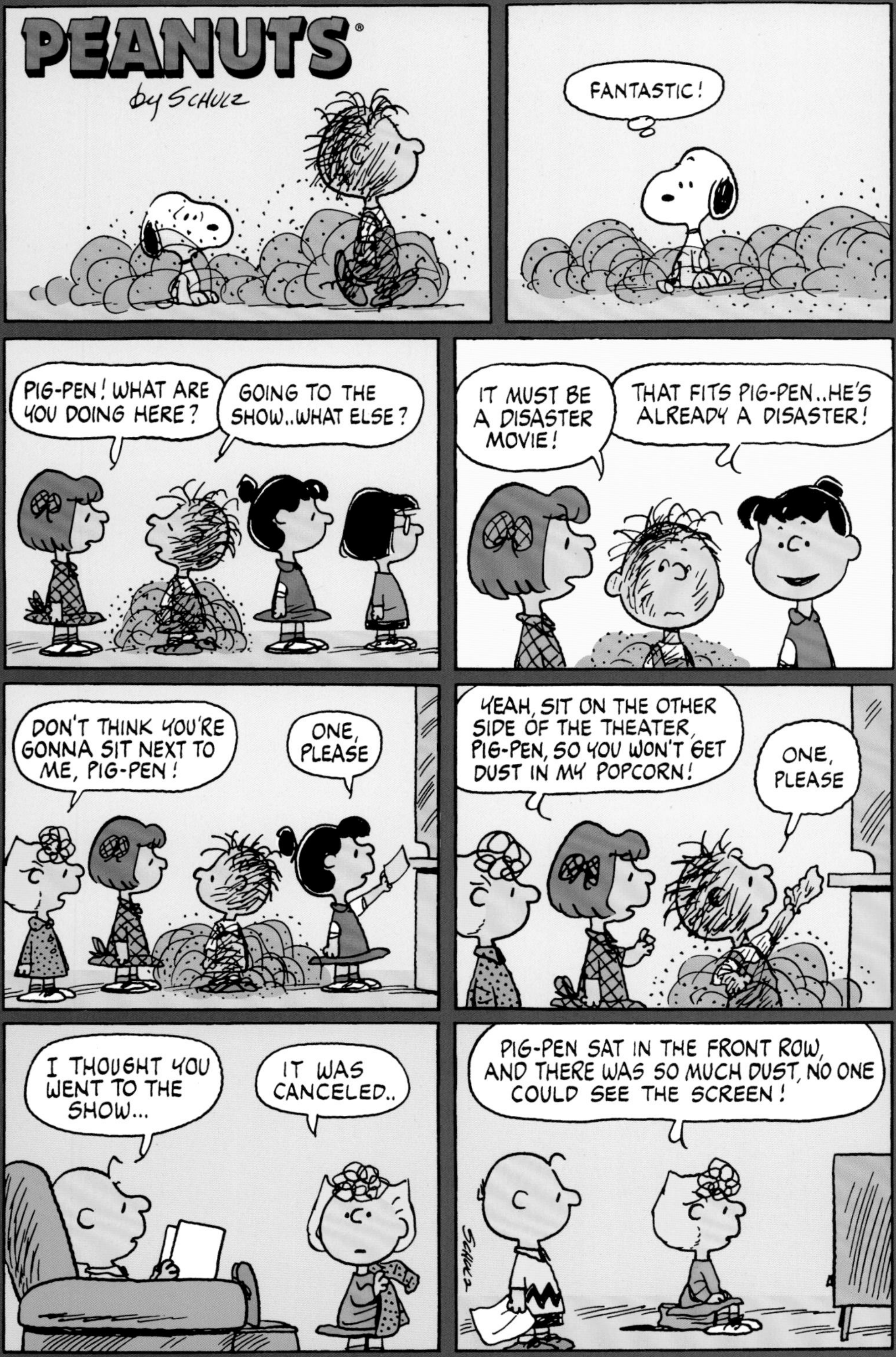
PEANUTS
by SCHULZ
FANTASTIC!
PIG-PEN! WHAT ARE YOU DOING HERE?
GOING TO THE SHOW..WHAT ELSE?
IT MUST BE A DISASTER MOVIE!
THAT FITS PIG-PEN..HE'S ALREADY A DISASTER!
DON'T THINK YOU'RE GONNA SIT NEXT TO ME, PIG-PEN!
ONE, PLEASE
YEAH, SIT ON THE OTHER SIDE OF THE THEATER, PIG-PEN, SO YOU WON'T GET DUST IN MY POPCORN!
ONE, PLEASE
I THOUGHT YOU WENT TO THE SHOW...
IT WAS CANCELED..
PIG-PEN SAT IN THE FRONT ROW, AND THERE WAS SO MUCH DUST, NO ONE COULD SEE THE SCREEN!
SCHULZ

POPCORN! POPCORN! GET YOUR POPCORN HERE! POPCORN!
3-25
ENJOY THE BALL GAME WITH A BAG OF POPCORN! GET YOUR POPCORN RIGHT HERE!
© 1981 United Feature Syndicate, Inc.
YES, MA'AM..TWENTY FIVE CENTS...THANK YOU.. ENJOY THE GAME...
ENJOY THE GAME THAT I'M NOT PLAYING IN BECAUSE I'M SELLING POPCORN! POPCORN! GET YOUR POPCORN!
SCHULZ

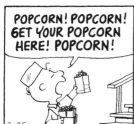

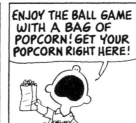

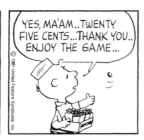

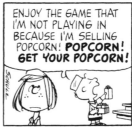

PIGPEN'S DUSTY POPCORN

Add your own dust cloud to your popcorn! You can use either sweet or savory "dust" for this snack—or you can have both.

INGREDIENTS

- 1/3 cup canola oil
- ½ cup popcorn kernels
- ¼ cup confectioners' sugar
- 3 teaspoons salt
- 1 cup grated Parmesan cheese
- 3 tablespoons unsalted butter, melted

Makes about 4 servings

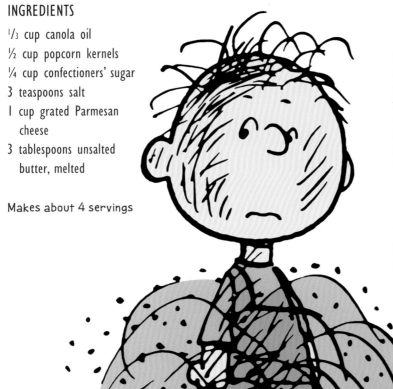

1 Pour the canola oil into the bottom of a large, heavy saucepan and heat over medium heat. Add the popcorn kernels, cover, and cook, shaking the pan often, until you start to hear popping. Continue to cook, shaking the pot continuously, until the popping slows to 3–5 seconds between pops. Remove from the heat and divide the popcorn evenly between 2 containers.

2 Sprinkle the confectioners' sugar and 2 teaspoons of the salt over one bowl of popcorn. Sprinkle the cheese, butter, and remaining 1 teaspoon salt over the second bowl. Using clean hands or a large spoon, toss each bowl of popcorn to mix the ingredients evenly. Transfer the popcorn into sandwich bags—sweet in one bag and cheesy in another. Store any leftovers in airtight containers for up to 2 weeks.

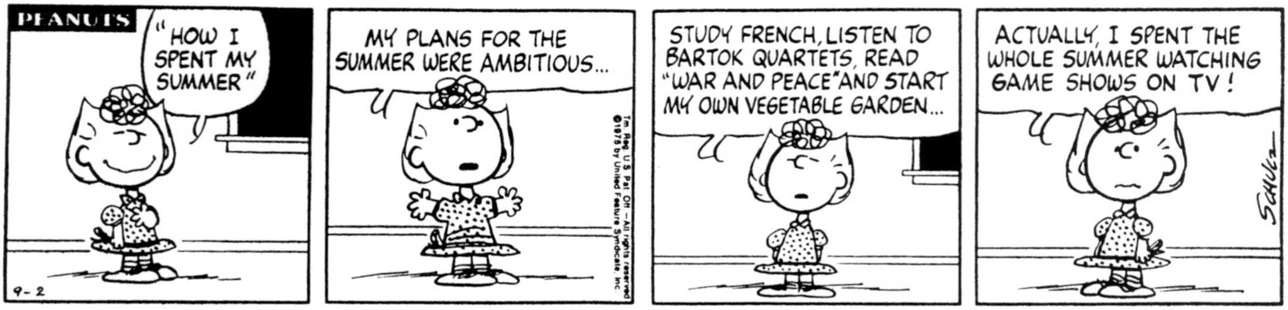
PEANUTS
"HOW I SPENT MY SUMMER"
MY PLANS FOR THE SUMMER WERE AMBITIOUS...
Tm. Reg. U.S. Pat. Off.—All rights reserved
©1975 by United Feature Syndicate, Inc.
STUDY FRENCH, LISTEN TO BARTOK QUARTETS, READ "WAR AND PEACE" AND START MY OWN VEGETABLE GARDEN...
ACTUALLY, I SPENT THE WHOLE SUMMER WATCHING GAME SHOWS ON TV!
SCHULZ
9-2

SALLY'S NO-BAKE NO-ENERGY BITES

If, like Sally, your ambition exceeds your motivation, you can recharge your batteries with these appetizing and invigorating energy bites.

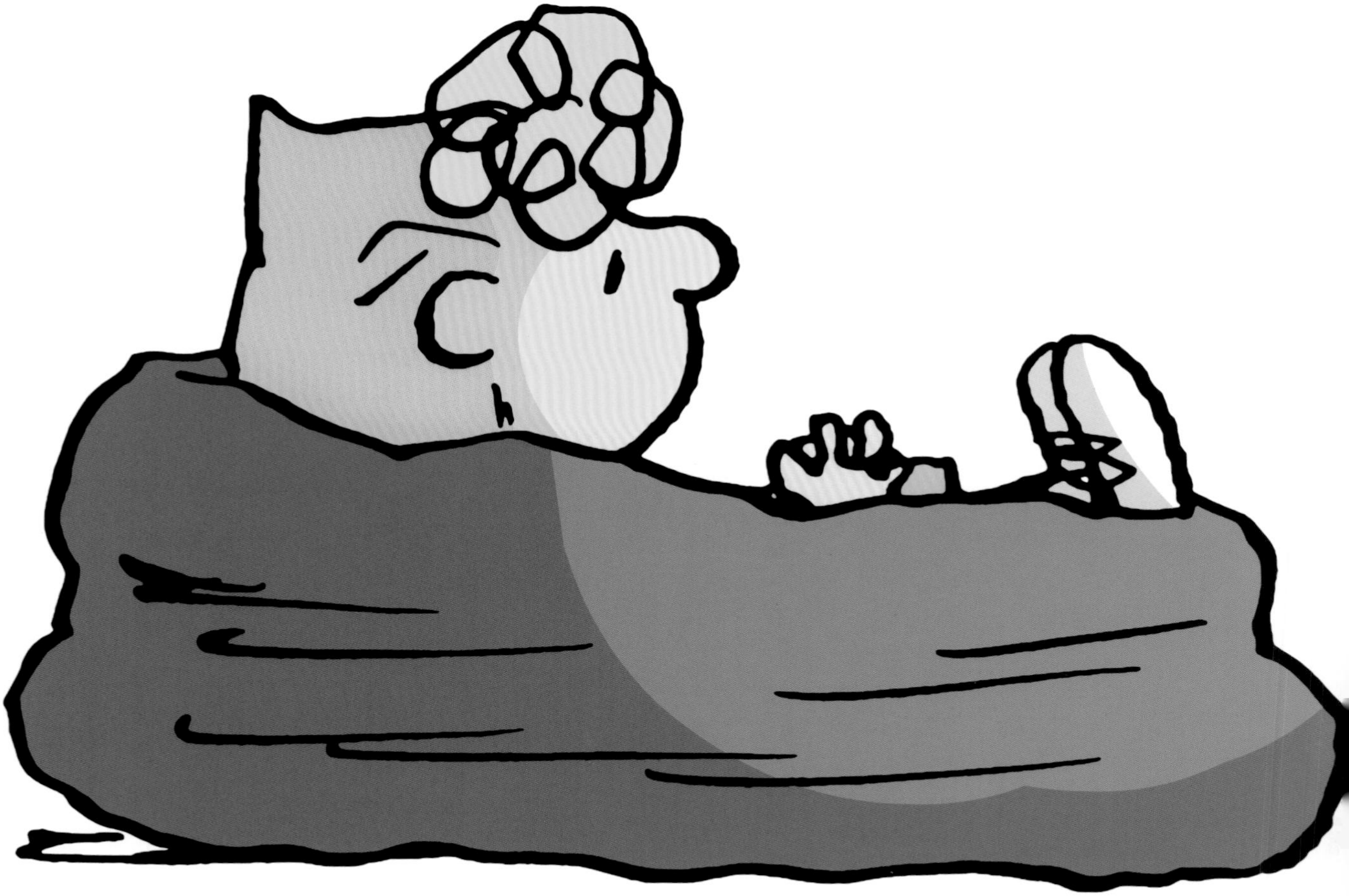

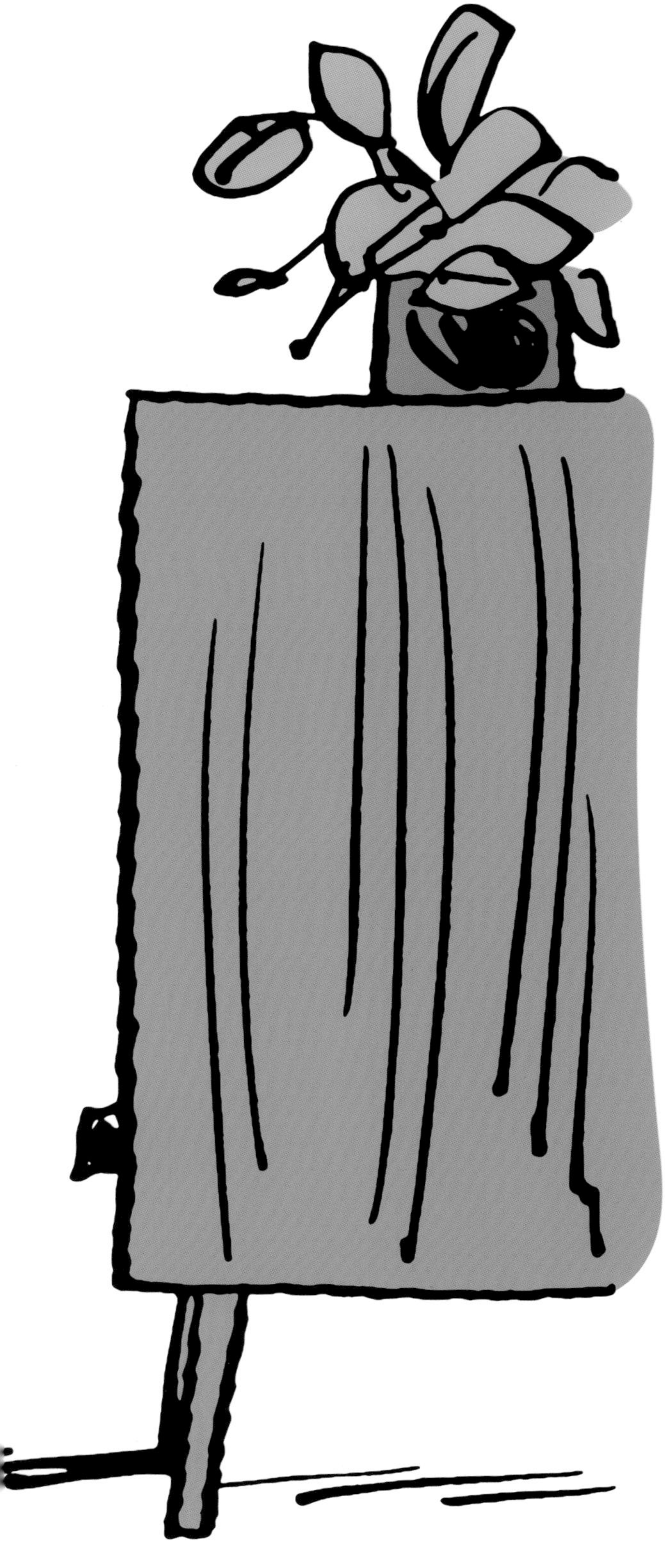

INGREDIENTS

- ¾ cup lightly packed chopped dried apples
- ½ cup pitted Medjool dates
- 1 teaspoon pure vanilla extract
- 1 teaspoon grated orange or lemon zest
- 1 cup lightly toasted nuts such as walnuts or almonds
- ¼ cup old-fashioned rolled oats
- 1 tablespoon pepitas or sesame seeds
- 1½ teaspoons ground cinnamon
- ¼ teaspoon salt

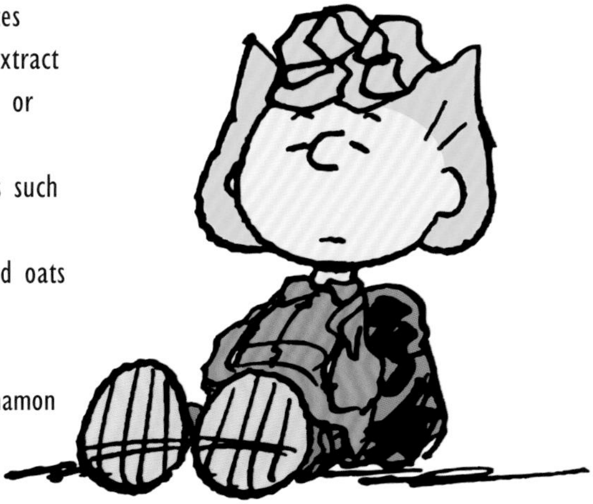

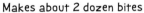

Makes about 2 dozen bites

1 Combine the apples, dates, vanilla, and zest in a food processor or blender and pulse until the mixture is well chopped and forms a ball, about 30 short pulses. Add the nuts, oats, pepitas, cinnamon, and salt and process until the nuts are finely ground and the mixture forms moist clumps when pressed together with your fingers, about 2 minutes.

2 Roll the mixture between your palms into ¾-inch balls. Pack in an airtight container, close tightly, and store for up to 5 days.

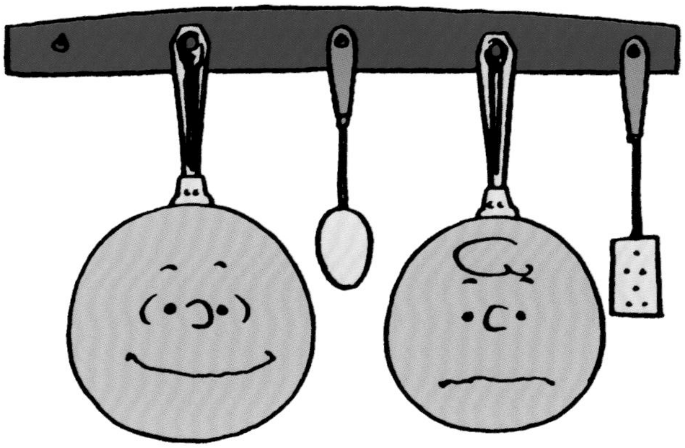

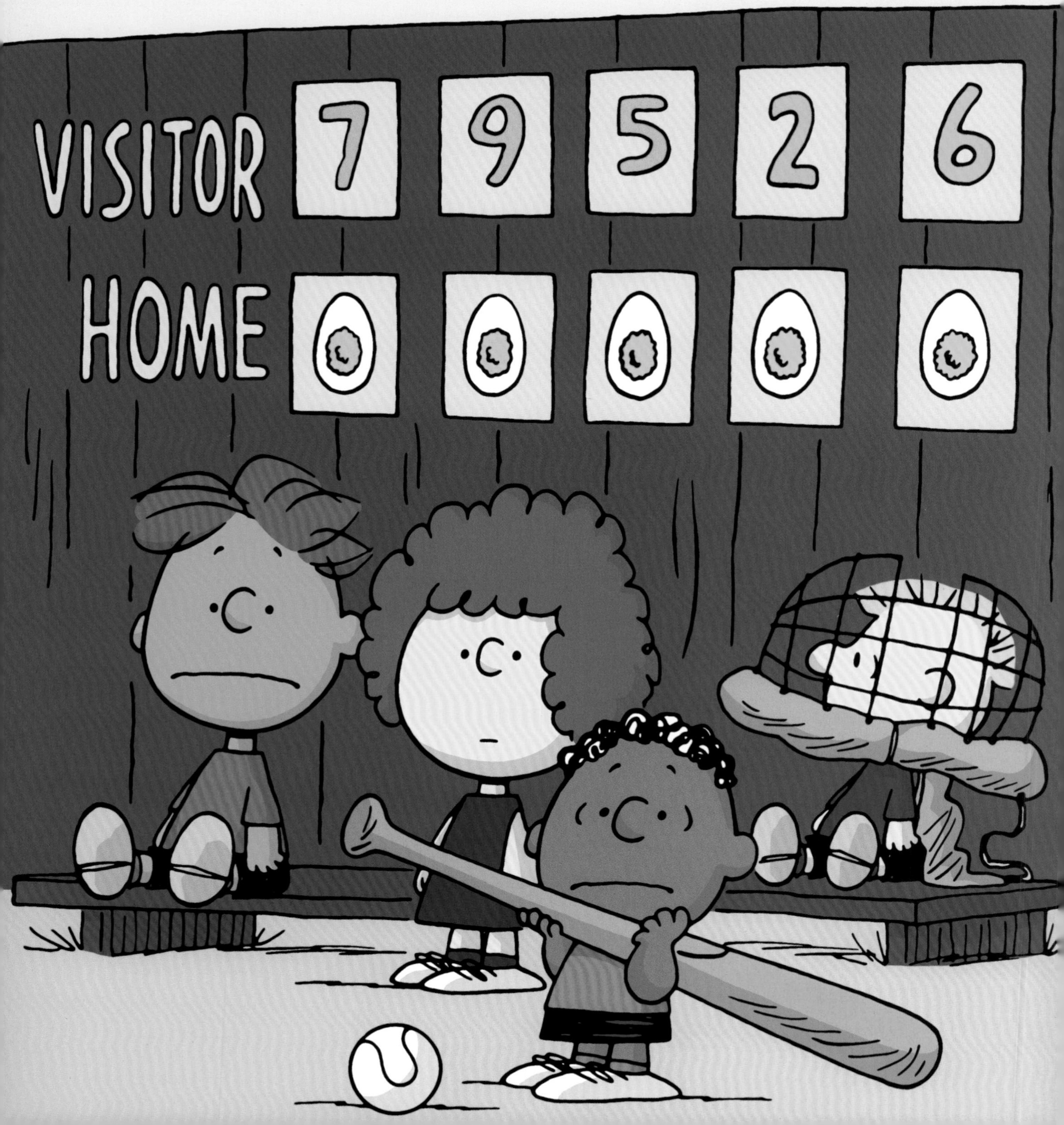
VISITOR 7 9 5 2 6
HOME

OKAY, AUSTIN... THIS IS THE PITCHER'S MOUND...
THIS IS WHERE YOU'LL STAND WHEN YOU PITCH THE BALL TO THE BATTERS
© 1977 United Feature Syndicate, Inc. 3-26
HOW DO I GET DOWN?
SCHULZ

DEVILED "GOOSE EGGS"

The little ones on the Goose Eggs baseball team may have a hard time holding up their bats, but they're big enough to enjoy the giant flavor of these deviled eggs.

INGREDIENTS

2 large eggs
1 tablespoon mayonnaise
¼ teaspoon Dijon mustard
Salt and freshly ground pepper
Paprika

Makes 4 deviled egg halves

1 Put the eggs in a small saucepan and add cold water to cover. Bring to a boil over high heat, then reduce the heat to medium-low and simmer the eggs for 12 minutes. Place the saucepan in the sink and run cold water over the eggs to cool them. Roll each egg on a work surface to crack the eggshell. Carefully peel the shell.

2 Cut each egg in half lengthwise. Using a spoon, scoop out the yolks and transfer to a bowl. Add the mayonnaise and mustard to the yolks. Use a spoon to mash them all together into a smooth paste. Season to taste with salt and pepper.

3 Carefully scoop a small mound of the yolk mixture back into each egg white half. Sprinkle each deviled egg with a small pinch of paprika. Pack in an airtight container and cover tightly. Refrigerate until ready to go, then pack in an insulated lunch cooler.

PEANUTS
THREE TIMES A DAY.
DAY AFTER DAY, WEEK AFTER WEEK, HE EATS THE SAME THING!
1-27
WHAT'S THAT?
PIZZA!
SIGH
SCHULZ

LUCY'S MINI PEPPERONI PIZZAS

Enjoy perfect contentment with the perfect snack—mini pizzas! Make it even better by mixing and matching your favorite toppings.

INGREDIENTS

- 1¼ cups lukewarm water (110°–120°F)
- 1 package (2¼ teaspoons) active dry yeast
- 1 tablespoon sugar
- 3 cups all-purpose flour, plus flour for dusting
- 1 tablespoon salt
- 2 tablespoons olive oil
- 1 jar (15 oz) tomato sauce
- 1 pound fresh mozzarella cheese, sliced
- Optional toppings: Sliced salami, mushrooms, bell peppers, olives, and basil leaves

Makes 4 mini pizzas

1 Pour the water into the bowl of a stand mixer fitted with the paddle attachment, sprinkle with the yeast and sugar, and stir gently. Let stand until foamy, 5 to 10 minutes. Add the flour, salt, and olive oil and beat on low speed until a rough, shaggy dough forms, about 5 minutes.

2 Transfer the dough to a floured work surface and knead until the dough is smooth and not sticky, about 5 minutes. Shape the dough into a ball. Put the dough in an oiled bowl and turn it to coat it with the oil. Cover the bowl with a kitchen towel. Let the dough rise until doubled in size, about 1 hour.

3 Punch down the dough. Divide it into 4 balls. Sprinkle a rimmed baking sheet with flour, place the balls on it, and cover with a kitchen towel. Let rise until doubled in size, about 30 minutes. Wrap any extra dough tightly in plastic wrap and store in the refrigerator for up to 1 week.

4 Preheat the oven to 500°F. Sprinkle the work surface with flour. Press each ball to deflate, then flatten and stretch it into a 10-inch round. Transfer the rounds to 2 rimmed baking sheets. Spread each with tomato sauce and top with cheese and other toppings of your choice.

5 Bake until the cheese has melted and the crust is crisp and golden, 10–15 minutes. Cut into wedges, let cool for 10 minutes, then transfer to an airtight container and close tightly. Refrigerate until ready to go, then pack in an insulated lunch cooler.

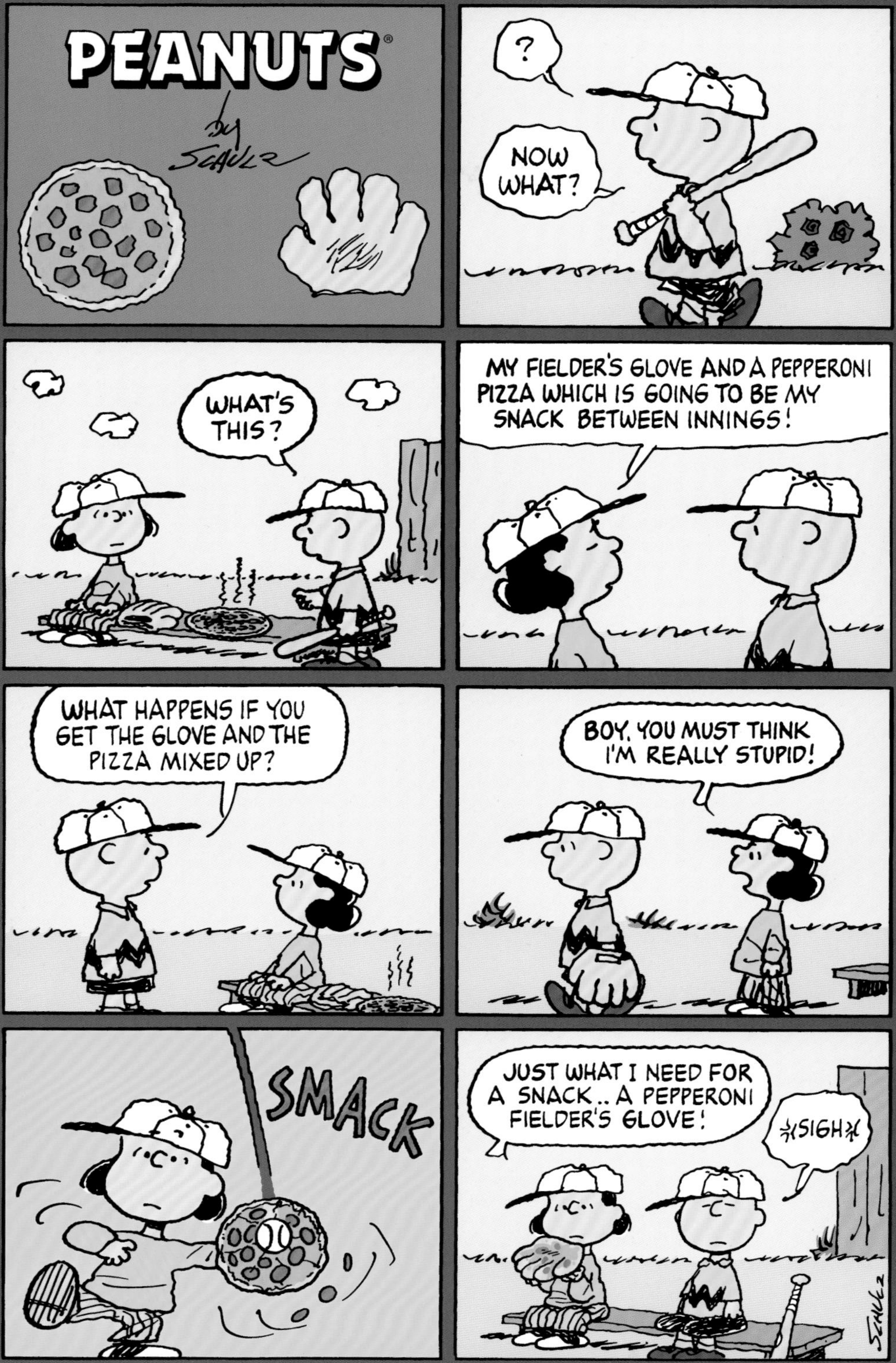
PEANUTS®
by SCHULZ
?
NOW WHAT?
WHAT'S THIS?
MY FIELDER'S GLOVE AND A PEPPERONI PIZZA WHICH IS GOING TO BE MY SNACK BETWEEN INNINGS!
WHAT HAPPENS IF YOU GET THE GLOVE AND THE PIZZA MIXED UP?
BOY, YOU MUST THINK I'M REALLY STUPID!
SMACK
JUST WHAT I NEED FOR A SNACK.. A PEPPERONI FIELDER'S GLOVE!
SIGH
SCHULZ

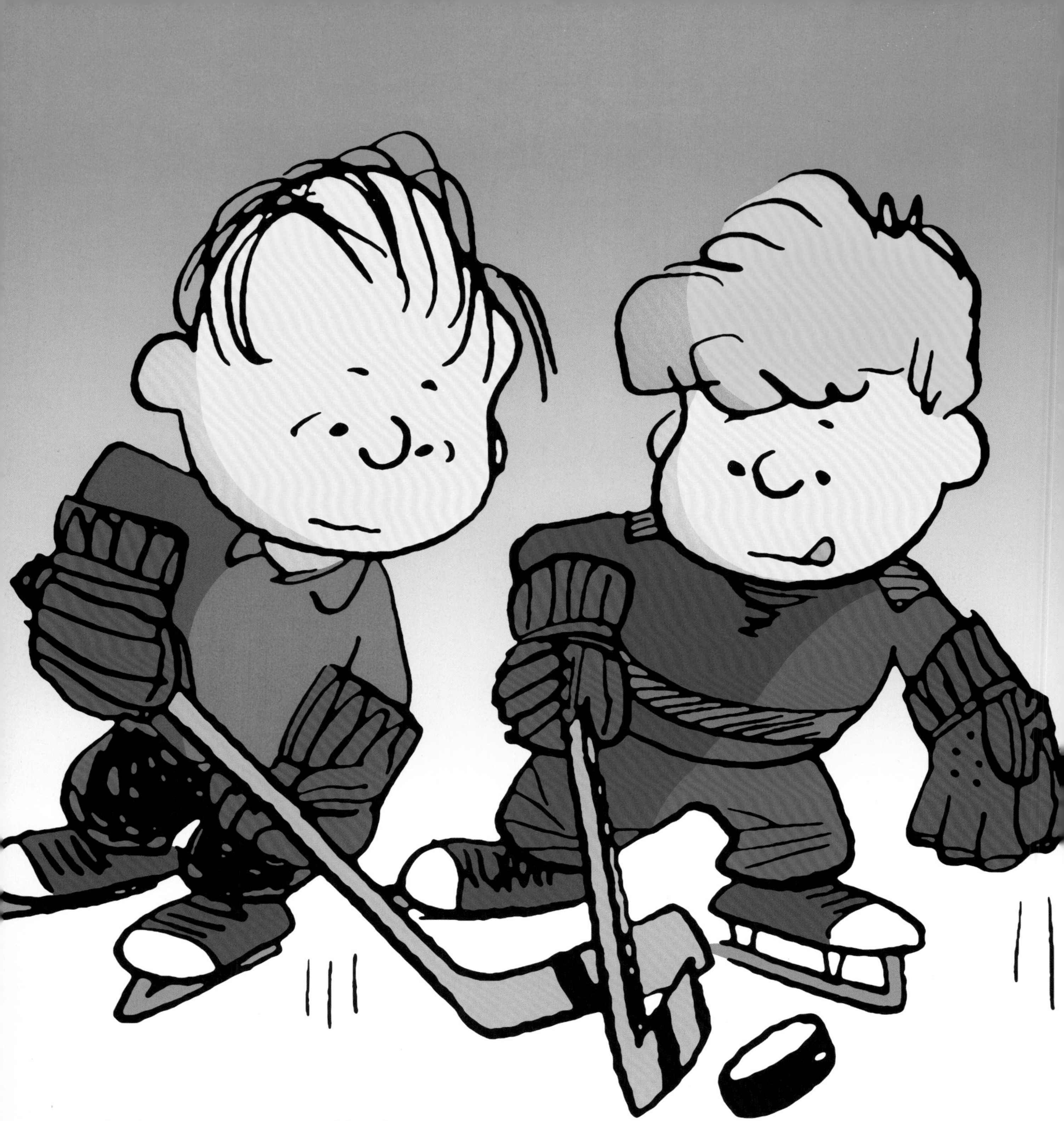

OFF TO PLAY HOCKEY, I SEE
© 1979 United Feature Syndicate, Inc.
THIS SHOULD BE A GOOD DAY FOR IT
12-26
CAN YOU CARRY THAT HEAVY BAG OF EQUIPMENT?
THIS ISN'T EQUIPMENT... THIS IS MY LUNCH!
SCHULZ

CHEESY HOCKEY STICKS

Score a hat trick with the sweetly textured yumminess of cornbread paired with Cheddar cheese!

INGREDIENTS

- 1 cup yellow cornmeal
- 1 cup all-purpose flour
- 3 tablespoons firmly packed golden brown sugar
- 1 teaspoon baking powder
- 1 teaspoon baking soda
- ½ teaspoon salt
- 2 large eggs
- 1 cup sour cream
- ¼ cup whole milk
- 4 tablespoons unsalted butter, melted and cooled slightly
- 1½ cups corn kernels, thawed if frozen
- ¼ cup shredded Cheddar cheese

Makes 4 to 6 servings

1. Preheat the oven to 425°F. Lightly grease a 9 x 13-inch baking pan. In a large bowl, stir together the cornmeal, flour, sugar, baking powder, baking soda, and salt. In another bowl, lightly beat the eggs, then whisk in the sour cream, milk, and melted butter until blended. Add the wet ingredients to the dry ingredients and stir until smooth. Stir in the corn kernels. Spread the batter evenly in the prepared pan. Sprinkle with the cheese.

2. Bake until the cornbread is golden brown and a toothpick inserted into the center comes out clean, about 20 minutes. Let cool slightly in the pan on a wire rack. Cut the cornbread into finger-size sticks, pack in an airtight container, close tightly, and store for up to 5 days.

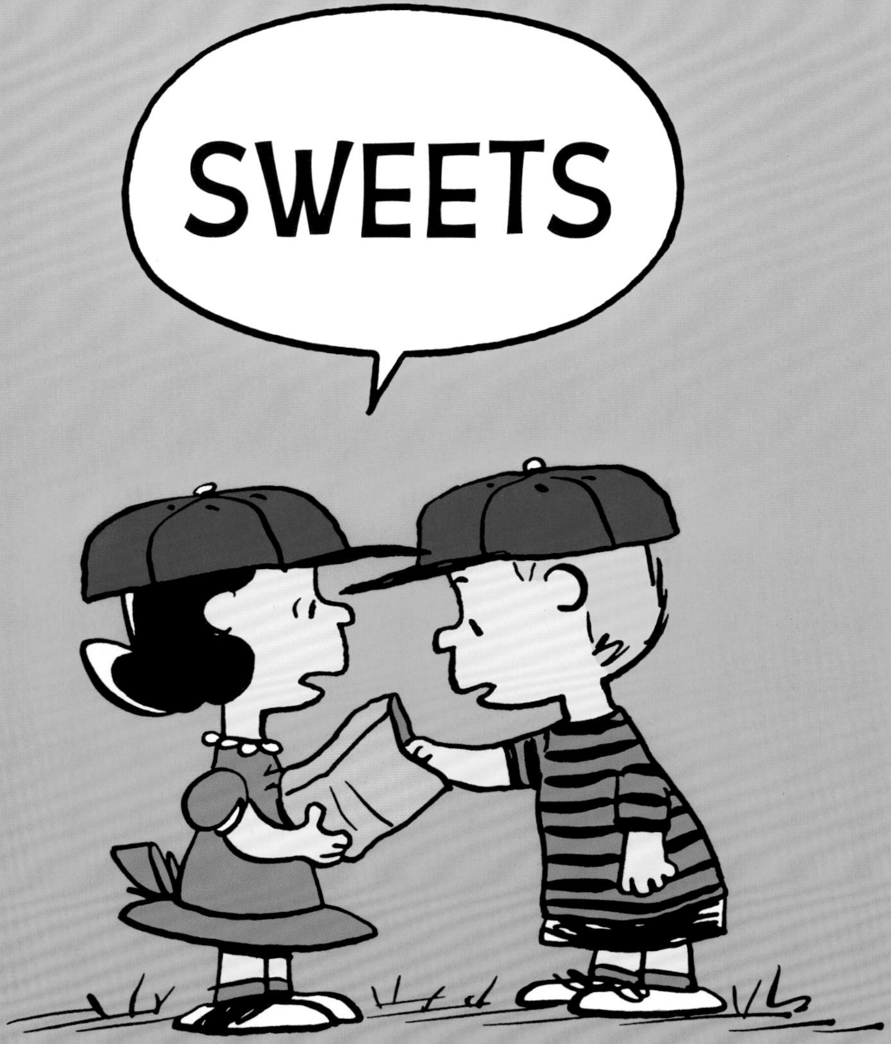
SWEETS

PEANUTS
SOME PEOPLE USE MONOFILAMENT LINE FOR FLYING THEIR KITES...
OTHERS ARE USING SMOOTH, BRAIDED SYNTHETICS LIKE DACRON AND NYLON...
SOME PEOPLE EVEN LIKE TO USE STEEL WIRE...
THIS IS STRANGE STUFF YOU'RE USING, CHARLIE BROWN.... WHAT DO YOU CALL IT?
STRING!

CHARLIE BROWN'S FRUIT KITES

The always-hungry Kite-Eating Tree will happily gobble up these sweet kite-shaped lemony berry bars. Choose the berry jam that you like best.

INGREDIENTS

½ cup (1 stick) unsalted butter, softened, plus butter for greasing
1¼ cups all-purpose flour
¼ cup confectioners' sugar
1 tablespoon ice water
1 teaspoon pure vanilla extract
¾ teaspoon salt
¾ cup raspberry or other berry jam
6 large eggs
2 cups granulated sugar
¾ cup fresh lemon juice
¾ teaspoon baking powder

Makes about 9 kites

1 Preheat the oven to 350°F. Butter a 9-inch square baking pan. To make the crust, in the bowl of an electric mixer fitted with the paddle attachment, beat the butter on medium speed until creamy. With the mixer on low speed, add 1 cup of the flour, the confectioners' sugar, ice water, vanilla, and ½ teaspoon of the salt and beat just until the mixture forms a ball.

2 Scoop the dough into the prepared pan and press to form an even layer over the pan bottom. Refrigerate for 10 minutes. Bake the crust until golden and firm, about 15 minutes. Let cool completely on a wire rack. Reduce the oven temperature to 325°F.

3 Using a silicone spatula, spread the jam evenly over the crust. In a bowl, combine the eggs, granulated sugar, lemon juice, remaining ¼ cup flour, baking powder, and remaining ¼ teaspoon salt. Whisk until smooth. Pour the egg mixture over the crust, spreading it with the back of the spatula to form an even layer.

4 Return the pan to the oven and bake until the top is set, 20–25 minutes. Let cool completely on a wire rack. Cut diagonally into "kites" or diagonals, pack in an airtight container, close tightly, and store in the refrigerator for up to 3 days.

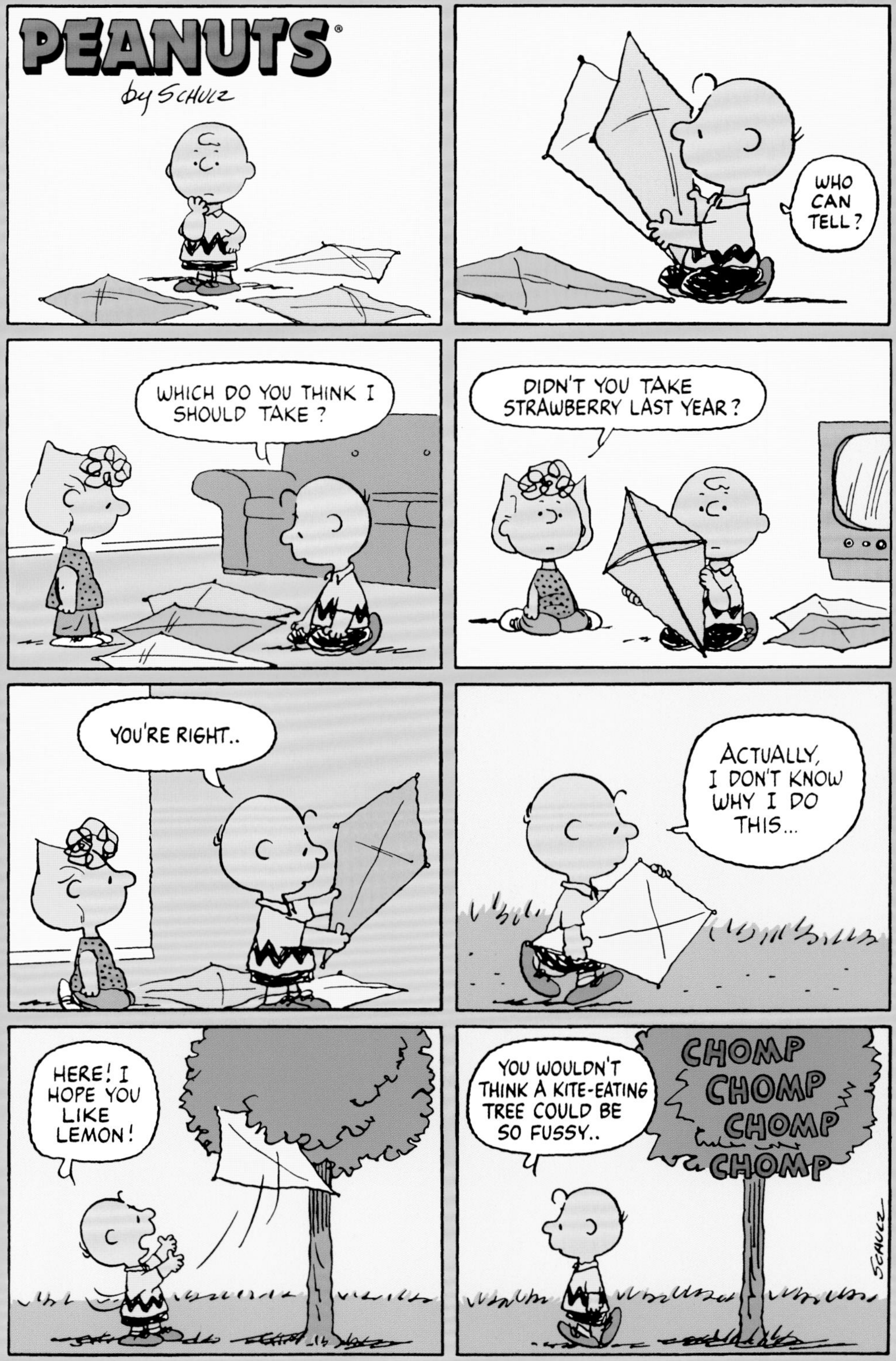
PEANUTS®
by SCHULZ
WHO CAN TELL?
WHICH DO YOU THINK I SHOULD TAKE?
DIDN'T YOU TAKE STRAWBERRY LAST YEAR?
YOU'RE RIGHT..
ACTUALLY, I DON'T KNOW WHY I DO THIS...
HERE! I HOPE YOU LIKE LEMON!
YOU WOULDN'T THINK A KITE-EATING TREE COULD BE SO FUSSY..
CHOMP CHOMP CHOMP CHOMP
SCHULZ

CHOMP
CHOMP CHOMP
CHOMP CHOMP
CRUNCH CRUNCH
CHOMP
PEANUT BRITTLE

"PEANUTS"
CHOMP CHOMP CHOMP
CHOMP CHOMP
CHOCOLATE CREAMS!
OH..
CHOMP CHOMP
CHOMP CHOMP
PEANUT BRITTLE!
SCHULZ
10-8

"CHOMP CHOMP" PEANUT BRITTLE

Enjoy the earsplitting crunch of peanuts encased in buttery caramel brittle.

INGREDIENTS

- 1 cup sugar
- ⅓ cup water
- 1¼ cups salted roasted peanuts
- 1½ tablespoons unsalted butter, softened
- ¼ teaspoon salt

Makes about ¾ lb brittle

1 Generously grease a rimmed baking sheet. In a small, heavy saucepan, combine the sugar and water. Set the pan over low heat and cook, stirring constantly, until the sugar dissolves. Using a pastry brush dipped in water, brush down the sides of the pan to prevent sugar crystals from forming. Raise the heat to high and bring the mixture to a rolling boil. Continue to boil, swirling the pan occasionally but without stirring, until the mixture turns a deep amber, about 8 minutes. (Be careful as the mixture will be very hot! Ask an adult for help if needed.) Remove from the heat.

2 Carefully add the peanuts, butter, and salt and stir until well combined with the syrup. Immediately pour the mixture onto the prepared baking sheet; be careful as the mixture will still be very hot! Using a wooden spoon, spread the mixture into a thin sheet, distributing the nuts evenly. Let cool completely. Break the brittle into irregular pieces. Pack in an airtight container, close tightly, and store for up to 2 weeks.

CHOMP! CHOMP!
CHOMP! CHOMP!
CHOMP!

PEANUTS | SURPRISE! | WHAT'S THIS? | FRENCH TOAST! I MADE IT MYSELF | BLEAH!! IT TASTES AWFUL! | REALLY? | MAYBE I SHOULDN'T HAVE MADE IT WITH CHOCOLATE MILK...

FRENCH TOAST STICKY FINGERS

Dip your "fingers" of French toast in a little blueberry–maple syrup. Just be careful you don't leave handprints all over the place.

INGREDIENTS

1 pint blueberries

³/₄ cup maple syrup

2 tablespoons sugar

1 teaspoon ground cinnamon

2 large eggs

½ cup buttermilk

½ cup whole milk

1 teaspoon pure
   vanilla extract

Pinch of salt

6 thick slices country bread,
   cut into 1-inch strips

2 tablespoons unsalted butter

Makes 4 servings

1 In a small saucepan, combine the blueberries and maple syrup. Bring to a boil over medium-low heat, stirring to prevent scorching, then remove from the heat and set aside to let cool. When cool, transfer to an airtight container and close tightly. Refrigerate until ready to go. In a large bowl, stir together the sugar and cinnamon.

2 In a large, shallow bowl, whisk together the eggs, buttermilk, milk, vanilla, and salt until blended. Place the bread strips in the egg mixture and, using a large spoon, toss gently until the strips are evenly coated and all the egg mixture has been absorbed.

3 In a large frying pan, melt 1 tablespoon of the butter over medium heat. Add half of the coated bread strips and cook, turning often, until golden brown on all sides, about 5 minutes. Transfer the strips to the bowl with the cinnamon-sugar and toss to coat. Repeat with the remaining 1 tablespoon butter and bread strips.

4 Arrange the French toast fingers in an airtight container and sprinkle with the remaining cinnamon-sugar. Refrigerate until ready to go, then pack along with the blueberry sauce in an insulated lunch cooler.

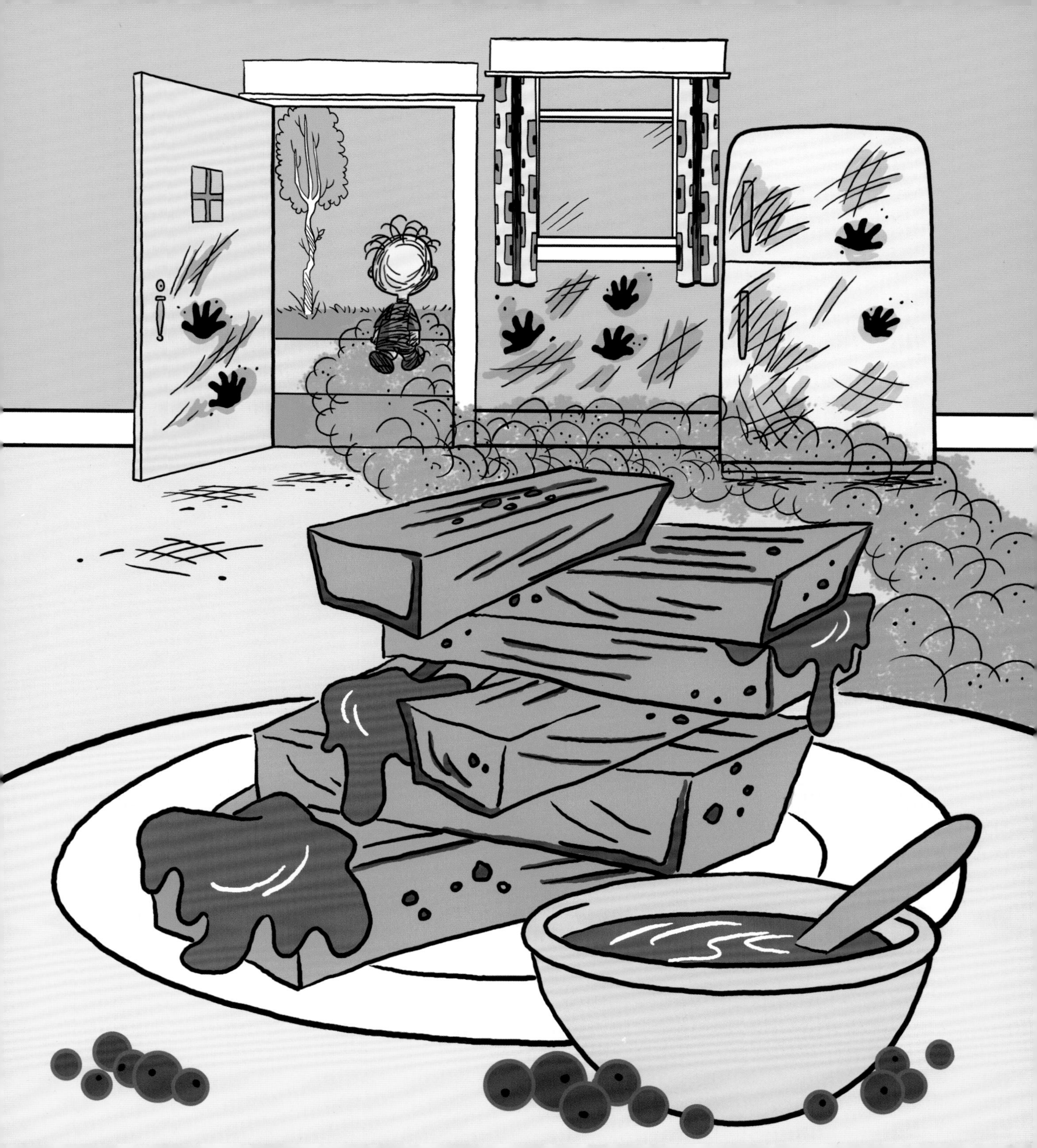

"PEANUTS"
YOU DON'T LIKE COCOANUT, DO YOU, CHARLIE BROWN?
CHOMP, CHOMP GOBBLE-GOBBLE
NO, I CAN'T STAND COCOANUT
I DIDN'T THINK YOU LIKED IT.. CHOMP CHOMP CHOMP GOBBLE-GOBBLE-GULP!
THOSE WERE CHOCOLATE CREAMS!
SCHULZ

GONE-BONS

These special treats for that extra-special occasion are so delectable, they won't last very long—savor the chocolaty flavor!

INGREDIENTS

12 oz milk chocolate, chopped

½ cup frozen orange juice concentrate, thawed

2 tablespoons unsalted butter, softened

Unsweetened cocoa powder for dusting

12 oz bittersweet or semisweet chocolate, finely chopped

Makes about 18 bonbons

1 In a heavy saucepan over medium-low heat, combine the milk chocolate and orange juice concentrate and stir constantly until smooth. Add the butter and stir until incorporated. Pour into a bowl, cover, and freeze until the mixture is firm enough to mound in a spoon, about 40 minutes.

2 Line a rimmed baking sheet with aluminum foil. Using a tablespoon, scoop out rounded spoonfuls of the frozen filling and drop onto the prepared pan, spacing them evenly. Cover and freeze until almost firm but still pliable, about 30 minutes.

3 Put the cocoa powder in a shallow bowl. Roll each chocolate mound between your palms into a smooth ball, then roll in the cocoa to coat evenly. Return to the baking sheet and freeze while you prepare the coating.

4 Line another rimmed baking sheet with foil. Put the bittersweet chocolate in the top pan of a double boiler or in a heatproof bowl. Place over (but not touching) a pan of barely simmering water and heat, stirring occasionally, until melted and smooth. Remove from the heat and let cool slightly.

5 Drop 1 truffle ball into the melted chocolate and tilt the pan if necessary to coat the ball completely. Slip a fork under the truffle, lift it from the chocolate, and tap the fork gently against the side of the pan to allow any excess chocolate to drip off. Using a knife, gently slide the truffle off the fork and onto the prepared pan. Repeat with the remaining truffles.

6 Refrigerate the truffles, uncovered, until firm, about 1 hour. Pack in an airtight container, close tightly, and refrigerate for up to 2 weeks.

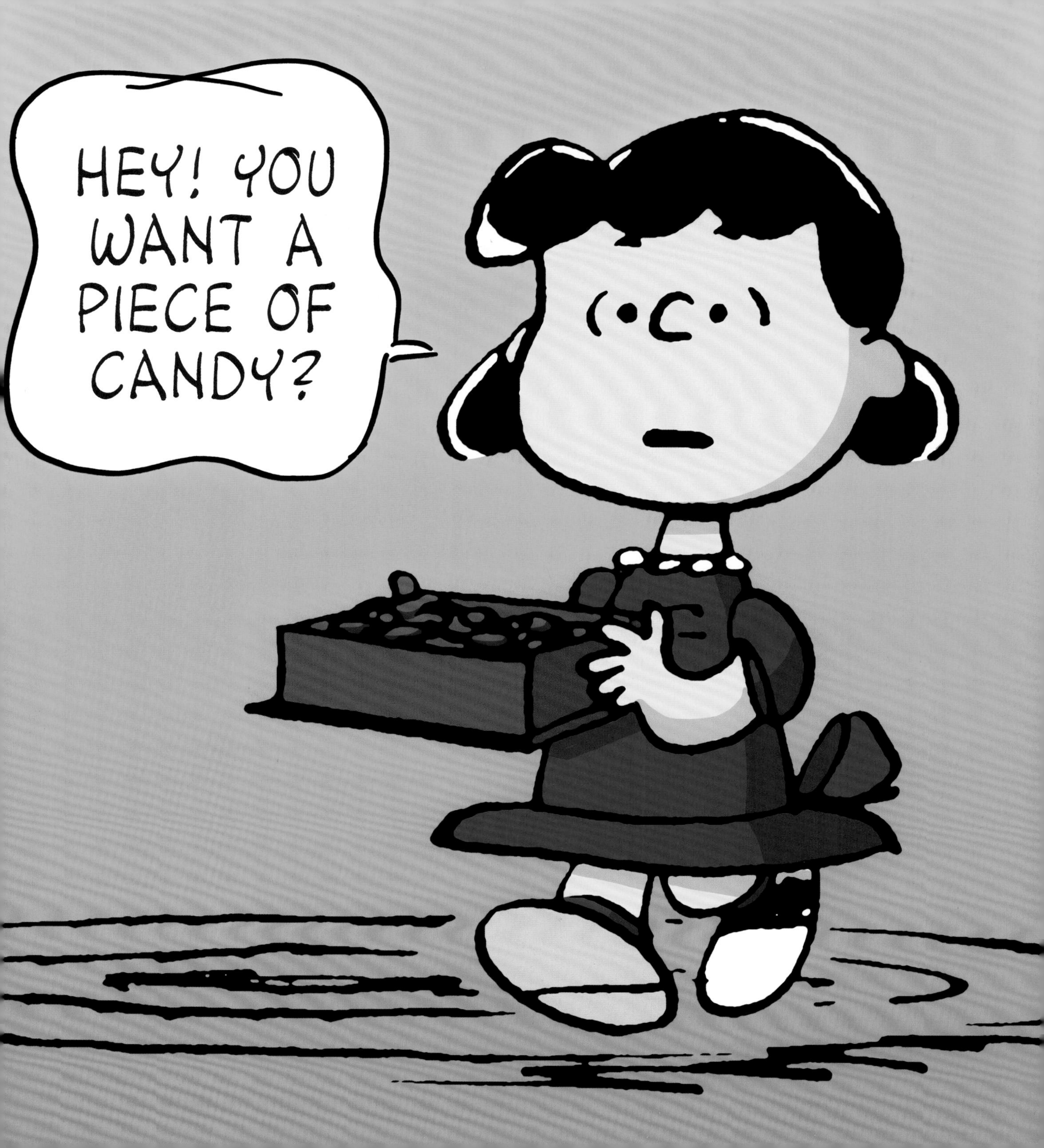
HEY! YOU WANT A PIECE OF CANDY?

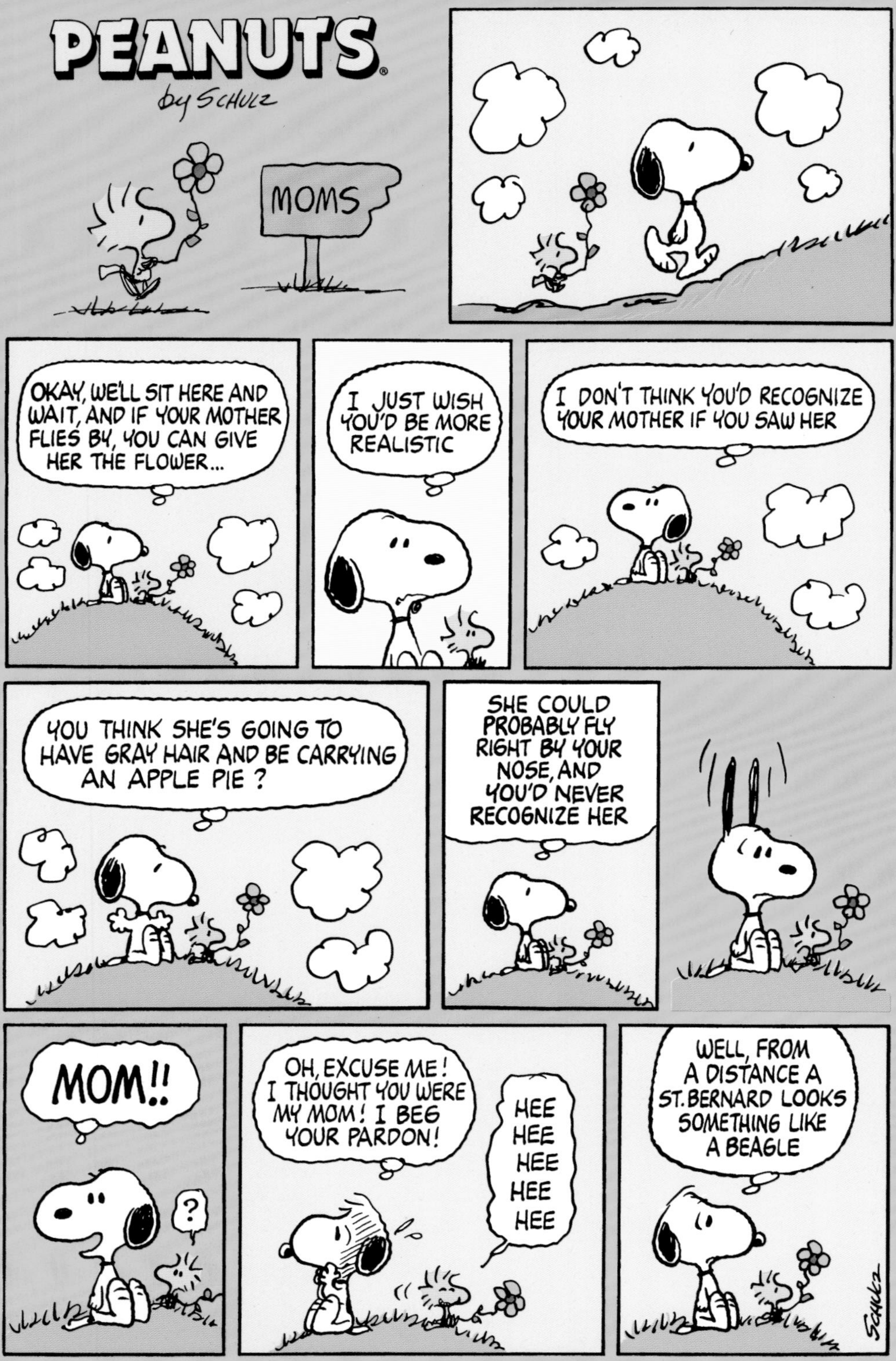

PEANUTS
by SCHULZ
MOMS
OKAY, WE'LL SIT HERE AND WAIT, AND IF YOUR MOTHER FLIES BY, YOU CAN GIVE HER THE FLOWER...
I JUST WISH YOU'D BE MORE REALISTIC
I DON'T THINK YOU'D RECOGNIZE YOUR MOTHER IF YOU SAW HER
YOU THINK SHE'S GOING TO HAVE GRAY HAIR AND BE CARRYING AN APPLE PIE ?
SHE COULD PROBABLY FLY RIGHT BY YOUR NOSE, AND YOU'D NEVER RECOGNIZE HER
MOM!!
?
OH, EXCUSE ME! I THOUGHT YOU WERE MY MOM! I BEG YOUR PARDON!
HEE HEE HEE HEE HEE
WELL, FROM A DISTANCE A ST. BERNARD LOOKS SOMETHING LIKE A BEAGLE
SCHULZ

"PEANUTS"
AND WHAT WOULD YOU LIKE TO HAVE FOR DESSERT, SIR?
WHAT KIND OF PIE DO YOU HAVE?
LEMON, PUMPKIN, APPLE AND PEACH!
OF COURSE, IT WON'T MATTER WHICH YOU ORDER...
THEY'RE ALL MADE OUT OF MUD!!
10/26
SCHULZ

MISSING MOM'S APPLE TART

Nothing says home like apple pie. When you need a little tender loving care, pack these sweet little tarts and keep comfort close by.

INGREDIENTS

All-purpose flour for dusting

1 sheet frozen puff pastry, thawed overnight in the refrigerator

2 Granny Smith, Braeburn, Fuji, or Cortland apples

4 tablespoons sugar

Makes 8 servings

1 Preheat the oven to 425°F. Line a rimmed baking sheet with parchment paper. Lay the puff pastry sheet on a lightly floured work surface and lightly dust the top with flour. Using a rolling pin, roll out the sheet to a 10 x 15-inch rectangle about ⅛ inch thick. Place the rectangle on the prepared pan and put in the freezer to chill while you prepare the apples.

2 Core the apples and cut them in half lengthwise. Slice each apple half into ¼-inch-thick half-moons.

3 Remove the pastry from the freezer. With a sharp paring knife, cut a 1-inch border along the edges of the puff pastry, being careful not to cut more than halfway through the pastry. Prick the pastry inside the border all over with a fork, then sprinkle evenly with 2 tablespoons of the sugar. Arrange the apple slices in slightly overlapping rows on the pastry inside the border and sprinkle the apples evenly with the remaining 2 tablespoons sugar.

4 Bake until the pastry is golden brown and the apples are tender, 15–20 minutes. Remove from the oven and let cool on the pan on a wire rack. Cut into pieces, arrange in an airtight container, close tightly, and store in the refrigerator for up to 3 days.

PEANUTS
MOM ALWAYS PUTS A NOTE IN MY LUNCH..
2-20
HMMM...
"A SMILE EACH DAY WILL BRING HAPPINESS YOUR WAY"
THAT'S NOT A LUNCH...IT'S A CHINESE FORTUNE COOKIE!
SCHULZ

FARON'S FORTUNE COOKIES

Fortune cookies are not just for takeout. Tuck words of wisdom and love into crispy, scrumptious cookies that even Frieda's cat, Faron, will love.

INGREDIENTS

¼ cup all-purpose flour
¼ cup sugar
Pinch of salt
1 large egg white
¼ teaspoon pure vanilla extract

Makes 12 cookies

MEOW

1. Preheat the oven to 375°F. Line a cookie sheet with parchment paper, then lightly grease the parchment.

2. Cut 12 strips of colored or white paper, each about 4 inches long by ½ inch wide. Write a fortune on each strip.

3. In a bowl, whisk together the flour, sugar, and salt. In a small bowl, whisk the egg white and vanilla until light and frothy, about 3 minutes. Add the egg white mixture to the flour mixture and stir with a wooden spoon until well combined. The batter will be thin.

4. Have ready a liquid measuring cup or mug and a muffin pan for shaping the cookies after baking. Scoop 1 teaspoon of the batter onto the prepared cookie sheet and, using a small icing spatula, spread it evenly into a circle about 3 inches in diameter. Repeat to create 3 more circles. Bake until the edges of the cookies are just starting to turn light brown but the centers are still pale, about 5 minutes. Remove the sheet from the oven and, using a metal spatula, move the cookies to a wire rack, turning them upside down.

5. Working quickly, place a fortune in the center of each cookie. Wearing an oven mitt, fold the hot cookies in half and pinch the edges closed. Press the straight edge of a cookie against the rim of the measuring cup and fold it over the rim to create a center crease. Place the cookie in the muffin pan so it keeps its shape. Repeat with the remaining folded cookies. Bake the remaining batter in 2 more batches and shape the cookies in the same way. Once cooled, pack the cookies in an airtight container, close tightly, and store for up to 3 days.

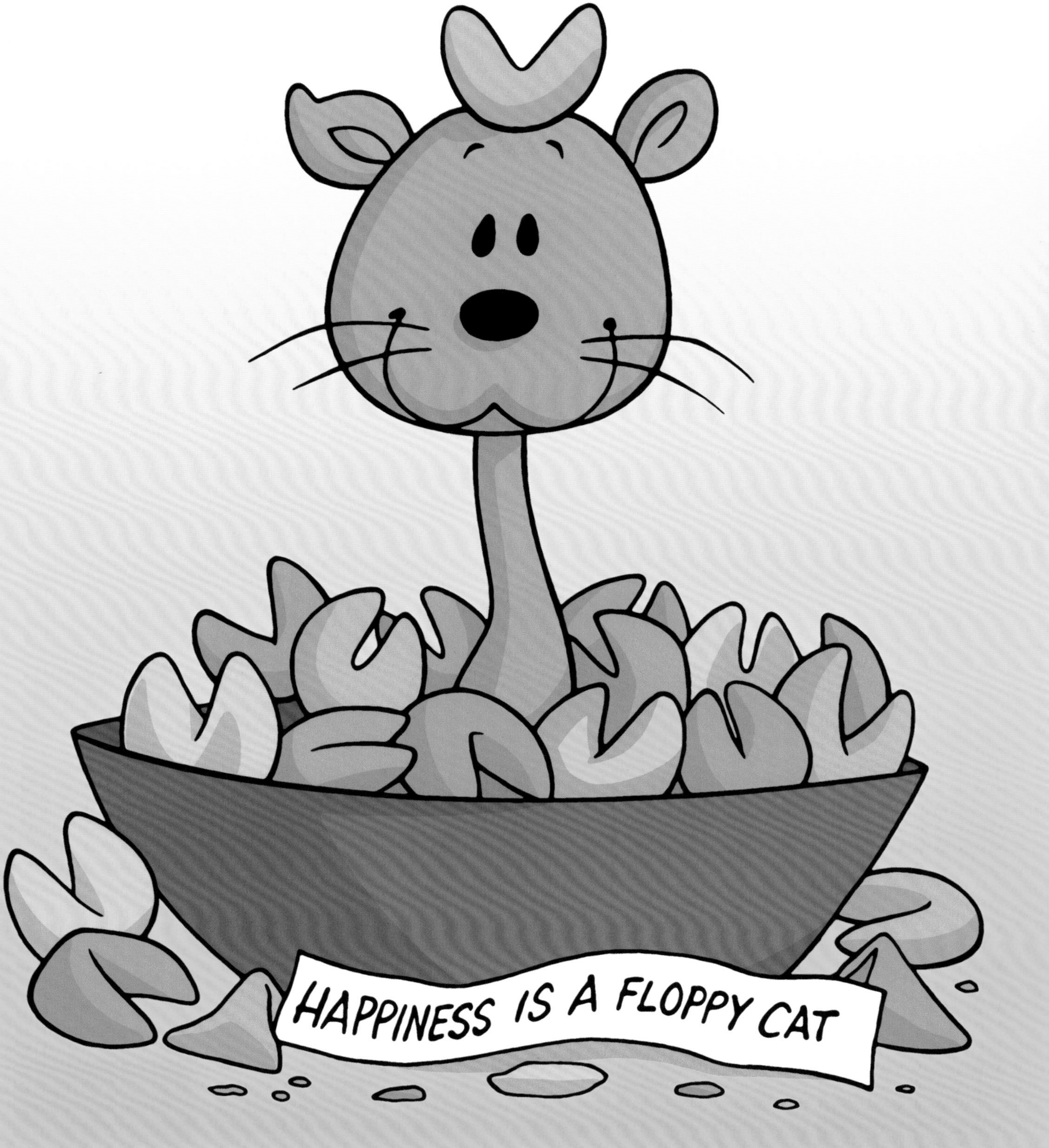
HAPPINESS IS A FLOPPY CAT

PEANUTS
Tm. Reg. U.S. Pat. Off.—All rights reserved ©1971 by United Feature Syndicate, Inc.
WHEE!
MERRY CHRISTMAS, OLD FRIEND..
WHEE! WHOOPEE!! WOW! RIGHT ON!
12-24
BLEAH!! EVERY TIME WE HAVE AN OFFICE PARTY, I DRINK TOO MUCH ROOT BEER!
SCHULZ

SNOOPY'S WHOOPEE! PIES

Equal parts cookie, cake, and pie, these soft cream-filled confections will have everyone shouting "Whoopie!"

INGREDIENTS

FOR THE CAKES:

2 cups all-purpose flour
1½ teaspoons baking soda
½ teaspoon salt
6 tablespoons unsalted butter, softened
½ cup firmly packed golden brown sugar
½ cup granulated sugar
1 tablespoon finely grated lemon zest
1 large egg
1 cup buttermilk
1 teaspoon pure vanilla extract
2 tablespoons nonpareil sprinkles
Nonstick cooking spray

1 Position 2 racks in the oven so that they are evenly spaced and preheat the oven to 350°F. Line 2 cookie sheets with parchment paper.

2 To make the cakes, in a bowl, whisk together the flour, baking soda, and salt. In the bowl of an electric mixer fitted with the paddle attachment, beat the butter and both sugars on medium speed until light and fluffy, 2–3 minutes. Turn off the mixer and scrape down the bowl with a silicone spatula. Add the lemon zest and beat on medium speed until combined. Add the egg and beat until blended. Turn off the mixer and add about half of the flour mixture. Mix on low speed just until blended. Pour in the buttermilk and vanilla and mix just until combined. Add the remaining flour mixture and mix just until blended. Turn off the mixer and scrape down the bowl. Using the spatula, gently fold in the sprinkles.

3 Spray a small ice-cream scoop (for standard whoopie pies) or a teaspoon (for mini pies) with nonstick cooking spray. Drop scoops of the batter onto the prepared cookie sheets, spacing them about 2 inches apart. Bake until the tops of the cakes are golden and firm to the touch, 9–10 minutes for standard pies or 8 minutes for mini pies. Set the cookie sheets on wire racks and let cool for 5 minutes, then use a metal spatula to move the cakes directly to the racks. Let cool completely, about 30 minutes.

FOR THE FILLING:

½ cup (1 stick) unsalted butter, softened

2½ cups confectioners' sugar

3 tablespoons whole milk

½ teaspoon pure vanilla extract

½ teaspoon lemon extract

Pinch of salt

Makes 15 regular or 30 mini whoopie pies

4 Meanwhile, to make the filling, in the bowl of an electric mixer fitted with the paddle attachment, beat the butter on medium speed until light and fluffy, about 2 minutes. Turn off the mixer and scrape down the bowl with a silicone spatula. Add the confectioners' sugar, milk, vanilla and lemon extracts, and salt and mix on low speed just until combined. Turn off the mixer and scrape down the bowl. Beat on medium-high speed until the filling is airy and smooth, about 5 minutes.

5 Fit a piping bag with a round tip or snip the corner from a plastic bag. Place the bag tip-end down in a glass and carefully spoon the filling into the bag using a silicone spatula, leaving about 2 inches free at the top. Gently twist the bag closed. Pipe the filling onto the flat side of one cake and top with another cake, flat side down, to create a sandwich. Repeat to fill and assemble the remaining cakes. Pack in an airtight container, close tightly, and store at room temperature for 1 day or in the refrigerator for up to 5 days.

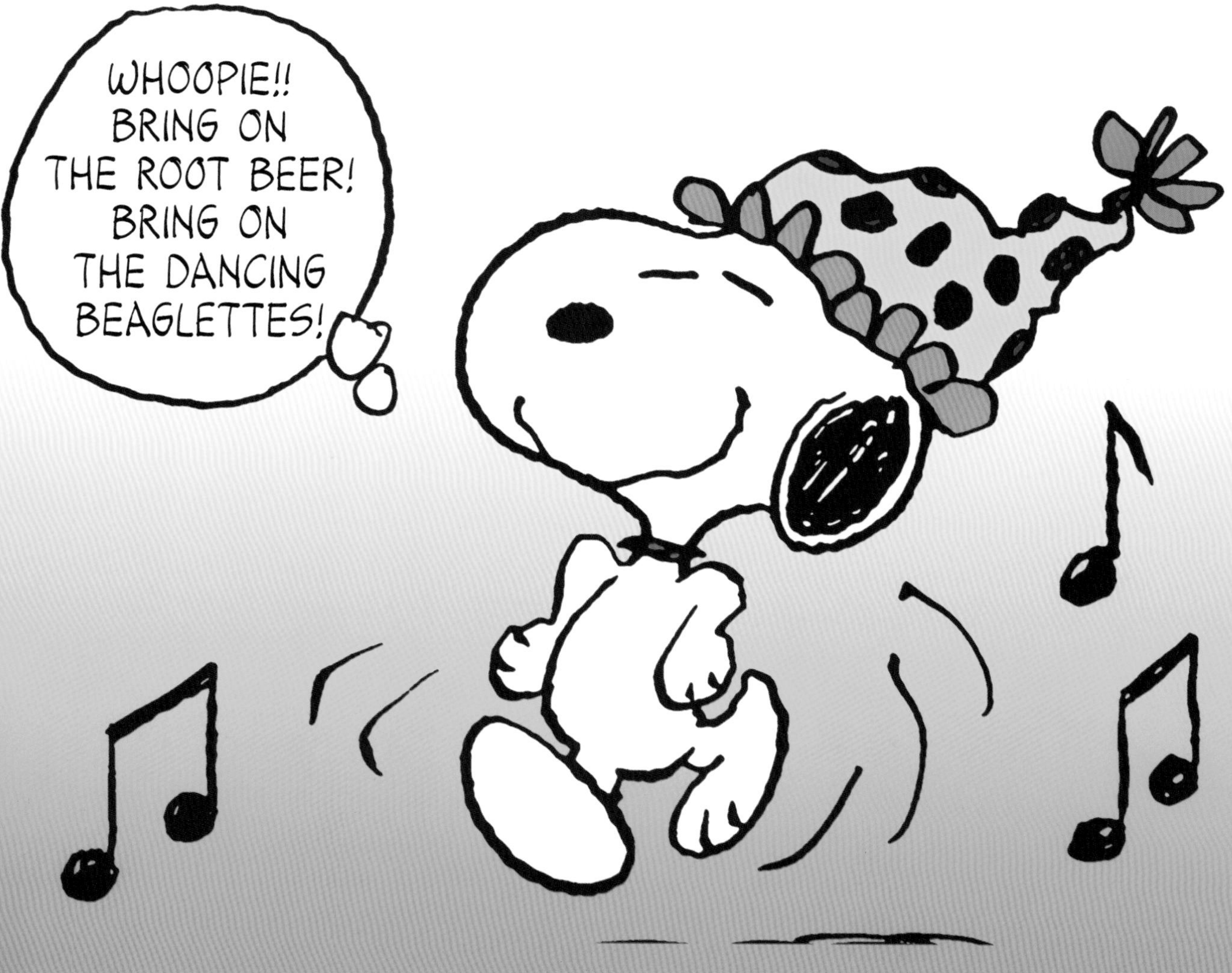
WHOOPIE!! BRING ON THE ROOT BEER! BRING ON THE DANCING BEAGLETTES!

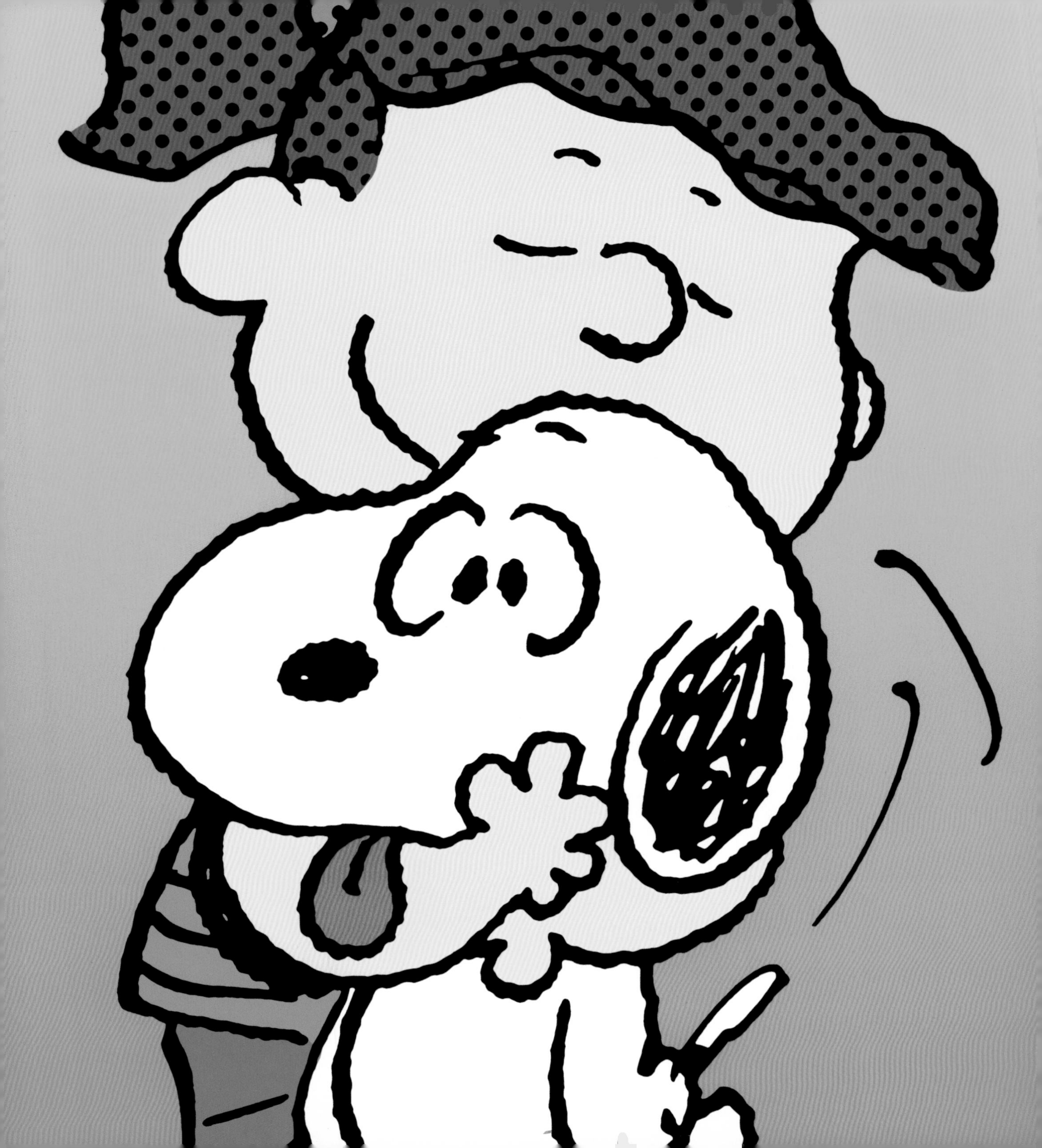

SQUEEZE...
SQUASH...
APPLESAUCE!!
WHEN YOU'RE FEELING LOW, NOTHING CHEERS YOU UP LIKE A FEW ROUNDS OF "SQUEEZE...SQUASH... APPLESAUCE!"
9-27
SCHULZ

SQUEEZE-SQUASH APPLESAUCE

You can squeeze another round out of your fall apple harvest by making homemade applesauce—a delicious, nutritious, and soothing standby.

INGREDIENTS

- 4 Fuji or Braeburn apples, peeled, cored, and coarsely diced
- ¼ cup sugar
- ¼ cup water
- 2 teaspoons fresh lemon juice
- Pinch of kosher salt

Makes 4 servings

1 In a saucepan, combine the apples, sugar, water, lemon juice, and salt and stir well. Bring to a boil over medium-high heat, then reduce the heat to low, cover, and simmer until the apples are tender, about 30 minutes. If the apples begin to dry out before they are ready, add a little more water. Uncover the pan and mash the apples lightly with a wooden spoon or a silicone spatula. Cook, uncovered, for 5 minutes to evaporate some of the excess moisture. The applesauce should be thick.

2 Let cool, then transfer to an airtight container and close tightly. Refrigerate any leftover applesauce in an airtight container for up to 5 days.

I CAN'T BELIEVE IT! I JUST SAW LINUS WALKING ALONG WITH THAT GRAPE JELLY PERSON!
HER NAME IS TAPIOCA PUDDING
9-12
© 1986 United Feature Syndicate, Inc.
TAPIOCA PUDDING! BLUEBERRY MUFFIN! WHAT'S SHE DOING WITH MY BOY FRIEND?!
I DIDN'T KNOW YOU WERE THE JEALOUS TYPE...
I KEEP IT ALL INSIDE!!
SCHULZ

SWEET BABLOOBERRY MUFFINS

As sweet as Sally's "Sweet Babboo," these blueberry muffins are so good, they could make even your taste buds jealous!

INGREDIENTS

2 large eggs
½ cup firmly packed golden brown sugar
⅓ cup canola oil
½ cup heavy cream
½ cup whole milk
1½ teaspoons pure vanilla extract
2¼ cups all-purpose flour
2 teaspoons baking powder
¼ teaspoon ground nutmeg
⅛ teaspoon salt
3 tablespoons unsalted butter, melted and slightly cooled
1½ cups blueberries

Makes 24 mini muffins

1 Preheat the oven to 400°F. Grease a 24-cup mini muffin pan or line with paper liners.

2 In a 4-cup glass measuring cup, whisk together the eggs, brown sugar, oil, cream, milk, and vanilla. In a large bowl, sift together the flour, baking powder, nutmeg, and salt. Make a well in the center and slowly pour in the egg mixture. Gradually mix into the dry ingredients until just combined. Add the melted butter and stir until almost smooth but still slightly lumpy. Do not overmix. The batter will be fairly thick. Gently fold the blueberries into the batter so that they are evenly distributed.

3 Spoon the batter into the prepared muffin cups, filling each about three-fourths full. Bake until a toothpick inserted into the center of a muffin comes out clean, 12–14 minutes. Let cool in the pan for 5 minutes, then turn out onto a wire rack and let cool completely. Arrange in an airtight container, close tightly, and store at room temperature for up to 3 days.

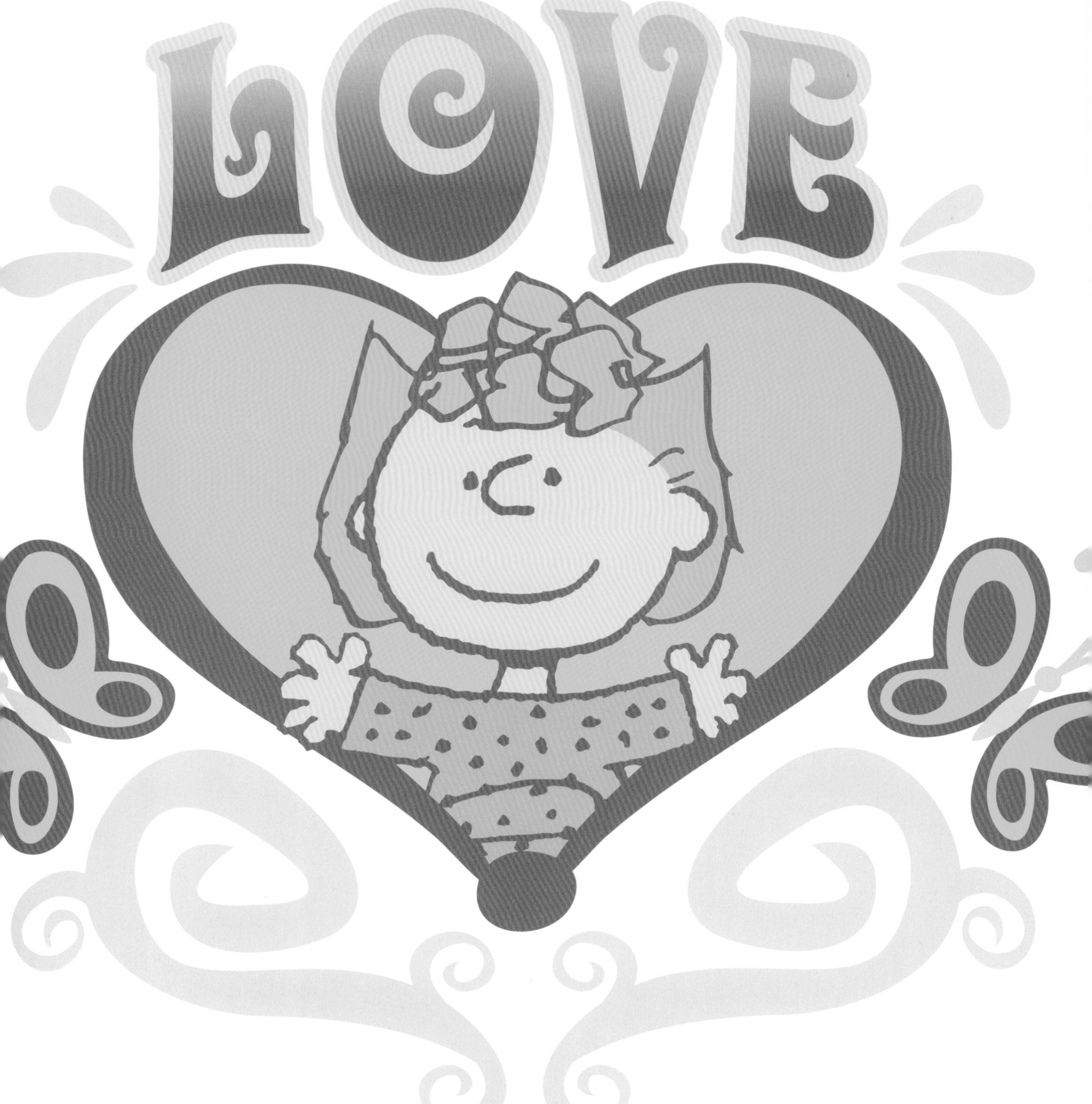
LOVE

ANYBODY HOME?
1-10-98
www.unitedmedia.com
© 1997 United Feature Syndicate, Inc.
THAT'S A GOOD IDEA... WHEN IT'S COLD, STAY IN YOUR IGLOO, AND BAKE CHOCOLATE CHIP COOKIES..
SCHULZ

WOODSTOCK'S MINI CHOCOLATE CHIRP MUFFINS

The next best thing to chocolate chip cookies? Chocolate chip muffins, of course!

INGREDIENTS

3 tablespoons poppy seeds
½ cup whole milk
1¾ cups all-purpose flour
2 teaspoons baking powder
½ teaspoon baking soda
¼ teaspoon salt
2 large eggs
¾ cup sugar
6 tablespoons unsalted butter, melted and slightly cooled
¼ cup orange juice
2 tablespoons mini chocolate chips

Makes 24 mini muffins

1 Preheat the oven to 400°F. Grease a 24-cup mini muffin pan or line with paper liners.

2 In a small bowl, combine the poppy seeds and milk and let stand for 20 minutes. In a bowl, stir together the flour, baking powder, baking soda, and salt. In the bowl of an electric mixer fitted with the paddle attachment, beat the eggs on low speed until blended. Add the sugar, butter, orange juice, chocolate chips, and the poppy seed mixture and beat just to combine. Add the dry ingredients and mix just until moistened.

?

3 Spoon the batter into the prepared muffin cups, filling each about three-fourths full. Bake until a toothpick inserted into the center of a muffin comes out clean, 12–14 minutes. Let cool in the pan for 5 minutes, then turn out onto a wire rack and let cool completely. Arrange in an airtight container, close tightly, and store at room temperature for up to 3 days.

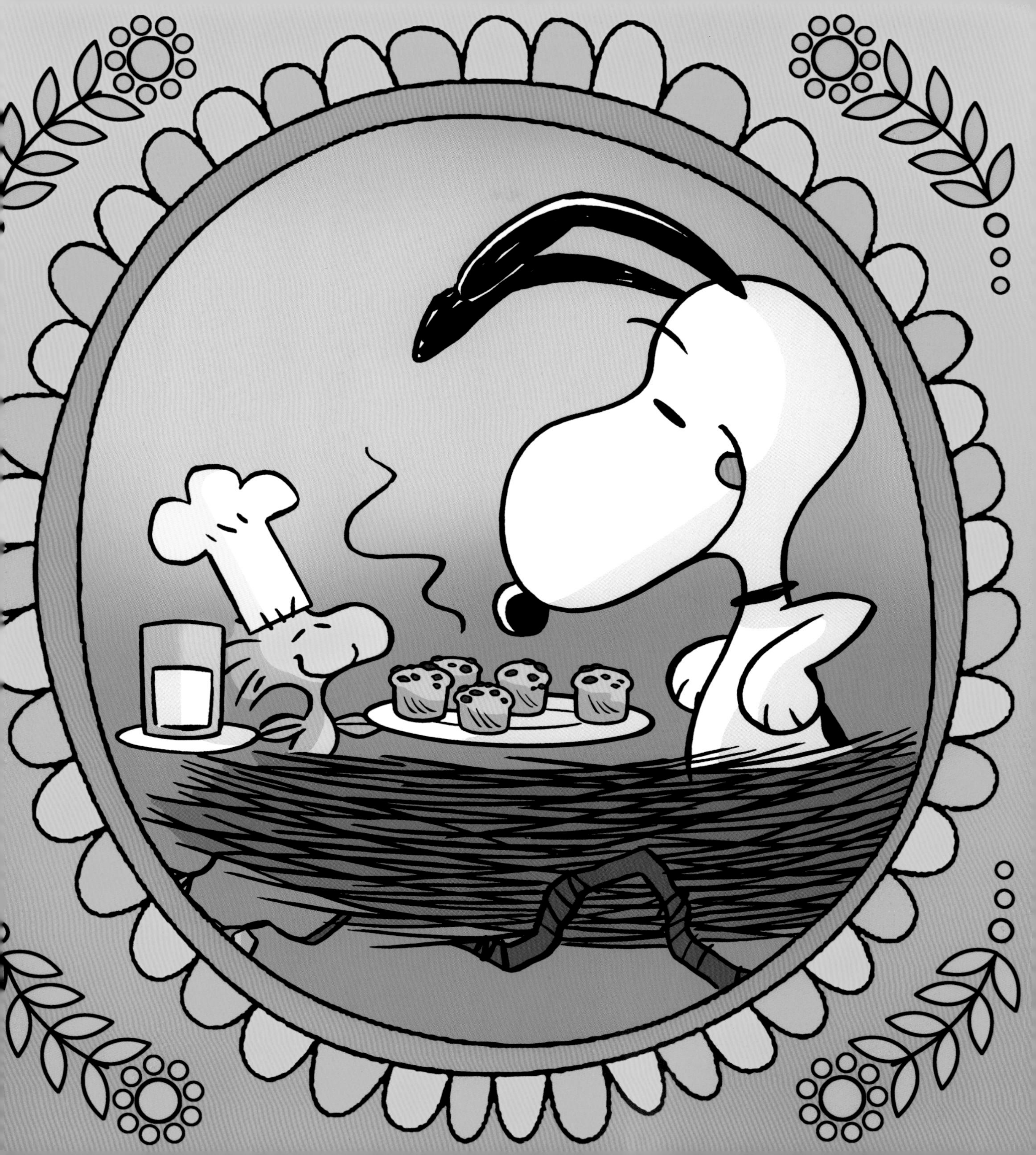

CONDIMENTS

Homemade Ketchup

INGREDIENTS

1 can (28 oz) crushed plum tomatoes
¼ cup light corn syrup
3 tablespoons apple cider vinegar
2 tablespoons minced yellow onion
2 tablespoons minced red bell pepper
1 small clove garlic, minced
1 tablespoon firmly packed brown sugar
1 teaspoon kosher salt
⅛ teaspoon freshly ground pepper
Pinch each of ground allspice, ground cloves, celery seeds, and yellow mustard seeds
½ bay leaf

Makes about 4 cups

In a heavy saucepan over medium heat, combine all of the ingredients. Bring to a boil, stirring. Reduce the heat to medium-low and cook at a brisk simmer, stirring frequently, until the mixture thickens and has reduced by half, about 1 hour. Rub the ingredients through a medium-mesh sieve into a heatproof bowl, discarding any solids. Let cool. Transfer to a container and refrigerate overnight to allow the flavors to blend. Store in an airtight container and refrigerate for up to 1 month.

Apple–Jicama Relish

INGREDIENTS

1 Granny Smith apple, cored and finely diced
¾ cup finely diced jicama
¼ cup finely diced red onion
2 tablespoons minced fresh cilantro
1 tablespoon extra-virgin olive oil
1 teaspoon apple cider vinegar
Salt and freshly ground pepper

Makes about 2½ cups

In a bowl, mix the apple, jicama, onion, cilantro, oil, and vinegar. Season to taste with salt and pepper. Store in an airtight container and refrigerate for up to 5 days.

Fresh Tomato Salsa

INGREDIENTS

3 tomatoes, finely chopped
1 small red onion, minced
2 jalapeño chiles, minced
2 cloves garlic, minced
3 tablespoons fresh lemon or lime juice
¼ cup chopped fresh cilantro
¼ cup olive oil
Salt and freshly ground pepper

Makes about 1½ cups

Stir together the tomatoes, onion, chiles, garlic, lemon juice, cilantro, and oil. Season to taste with salt and pepper. Store in an airtight container and refrigerate for up to 5 days.

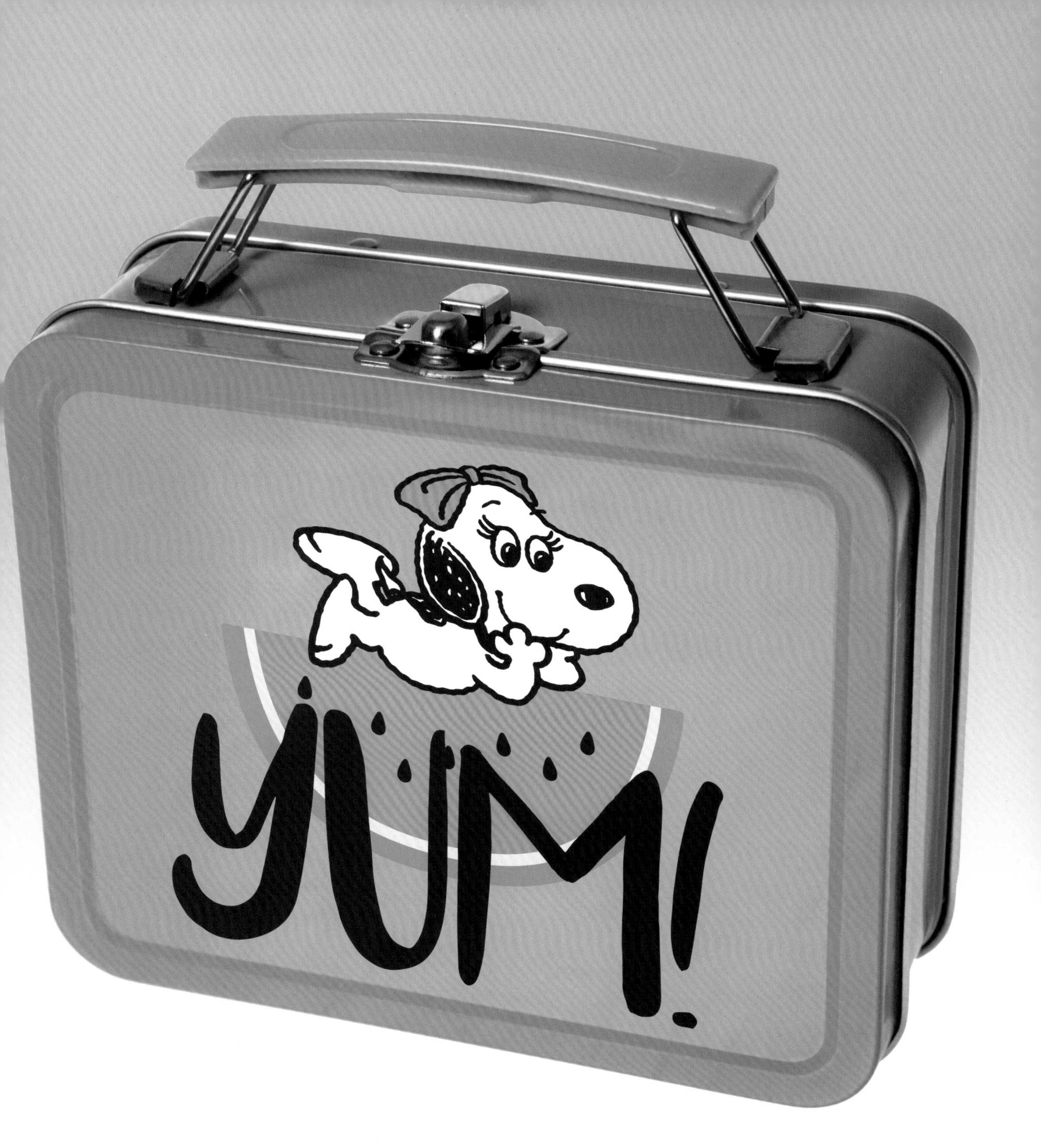
YUM!

INDEX

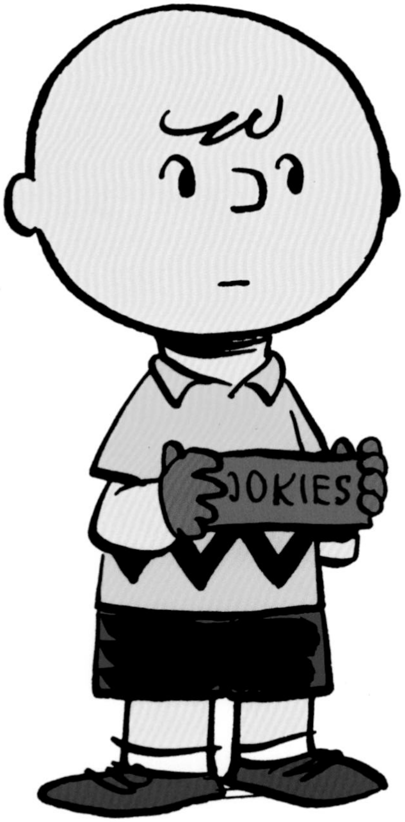
JOKIES

D

E

F

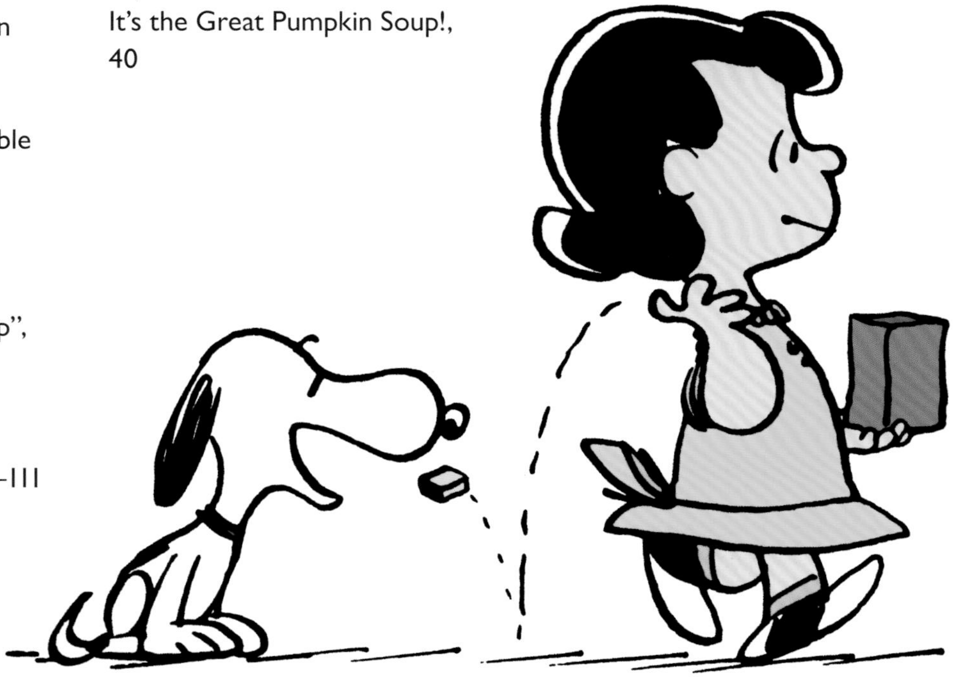

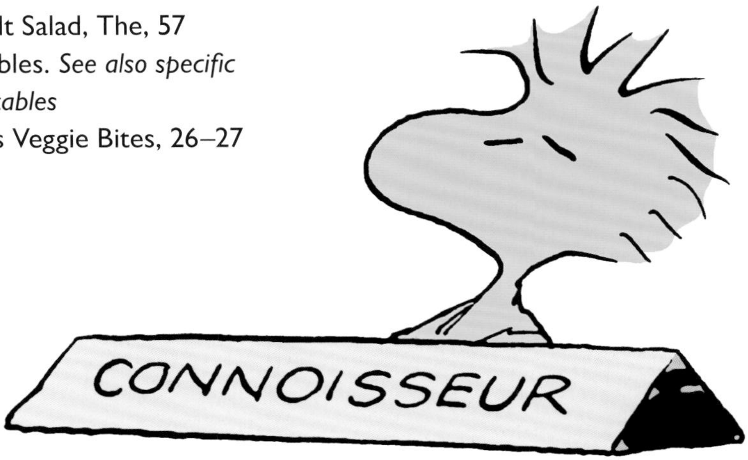
CONNOISSEUR

CREDITS

CHARLES M. SCHULZ is the artist for all strips, panels, and excerpts appearing in this book, unless otherwise cited.

ROBERT POPE: pages 25, 42, 70, 90, 109, 117

SCOTT JERALDS: pages 22, 31, 52, 80, 103

VICKI SCOTT: pages 4–5, 9, 35

weldon**owen**

Weldon Owen International
1150 Brickyard Cove Road, Richmond, CA 94801
www.weldonowen.com

PEANUTS
by SCHULZ
LUNCH TIME, SIR..
GOOD!
MOVE OVER, LITTLE GIRLS..LET A MAN SIT DOWN!
GIRLS TAKE UP TOO MUCH ROOM.. GIRLS ARE ALWAYS IN THE WAY...
MIRIAM WAS MOSES' OLDER SISTER.. IN CHAPTER TWELVE OF THE BOOK OF "NUMBERS" SHE ASKS, "HAS THE LORD SPOKEN ONLY THROUGH MOSES?"
WHAT'S THAT SUPPOSED TO MEAN?
I'LL EXPLAIN IT TO HIM, MARCIE...
POW!
HAM AND CHEESE TODAY, SIR..
PEANUT BUTTER AGAIN, MARCIE
MOSES? WHO WAS MOSES?
SCHULZ

CEO Raoul Goff
President Kate Jerome
Publisher Roger Shaw
Associate Publisher Amy Marr
Editorial Assistant Jourdan Plautz
Production Director Tarji Rodriquez
Production Manager Binh Au

Weldon Owen would like to thank Charles M. Schulz for bringing laughter to so many. Heartfelt thanks also to all the folks at CAMERON + COMPANY who have worked with such wonderful creativity and diligence in producing this book.

Library of Congress Cataloging-in-Publication data is available.

ISBN: 978-1-68188-572-8 • Printed in China
10 9 8 7 6 5 4 3 2 1 • 2020 2021 2022 2023

Produced in conjunction with CAMERON + COMPANY
Suite 7, 149 Kentucky Street, Petaluma, CA 94952
www.cameronbooks.com

Publisher Chris Gruener
Creative Director Iain Morris
Designer Emily Studer
Design Assistant Amy Wheless
Managing Editor Jan Hughes
Editorial Assistant Mason Harper

CAMERON + COMPANY would first and foremost like to thank Charles M. Schulz for bringing Peanuts into the world. We would also like to thank Peanuts Worldwide LLC and Charles M. Schulz Creative Associates for keeping his legacy alive and for their invaluable help with this project—special thanks to Senior Editor Alexis E. Fajardo for his tireless efforts on this project. Thank you to Karen Wise for copy editing. And a resounding thank-you to Roger Shaw, Amy Marr, and Jourdan Plautz at Weldon Owen, for making this book possible.

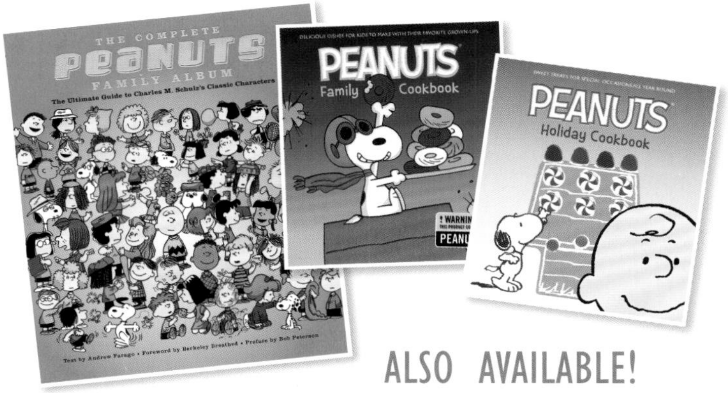
THE COMPLETE
PEANUTS
FAMILY ALBUM
The Ultimate Guide to Charles M. Schulz's Classic Characters
PEANUTS
Family Cookbook
PEANUTS
Holiday Cookbook

ALSO AVAILABLE!

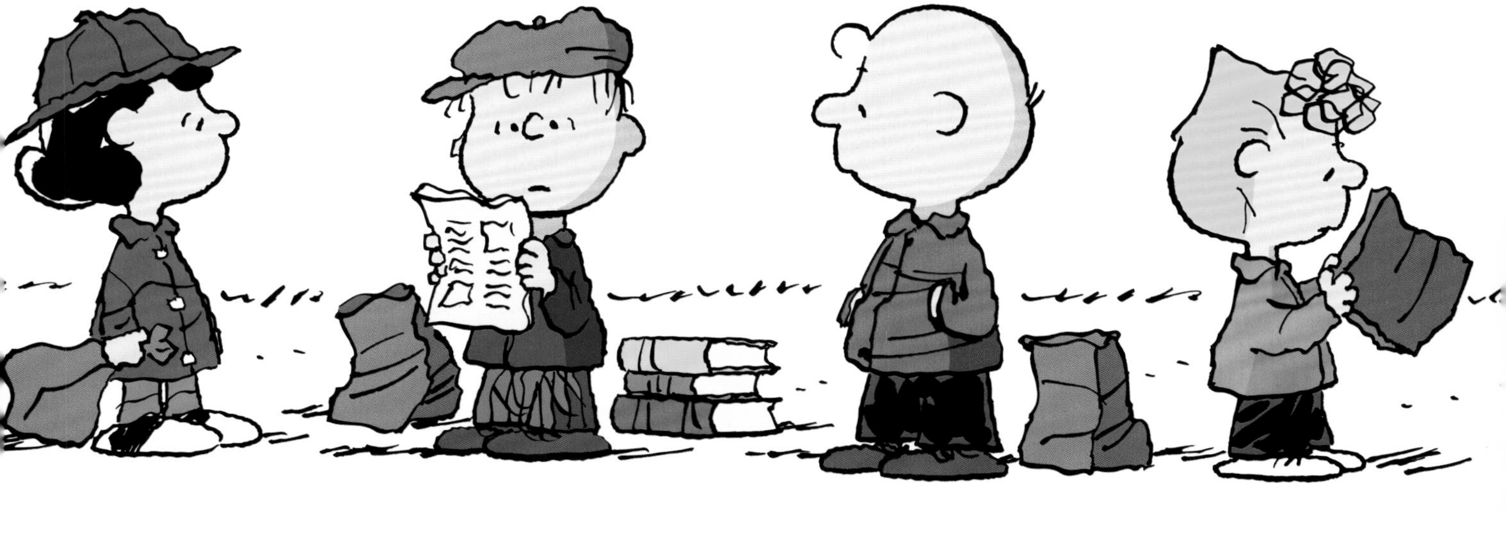

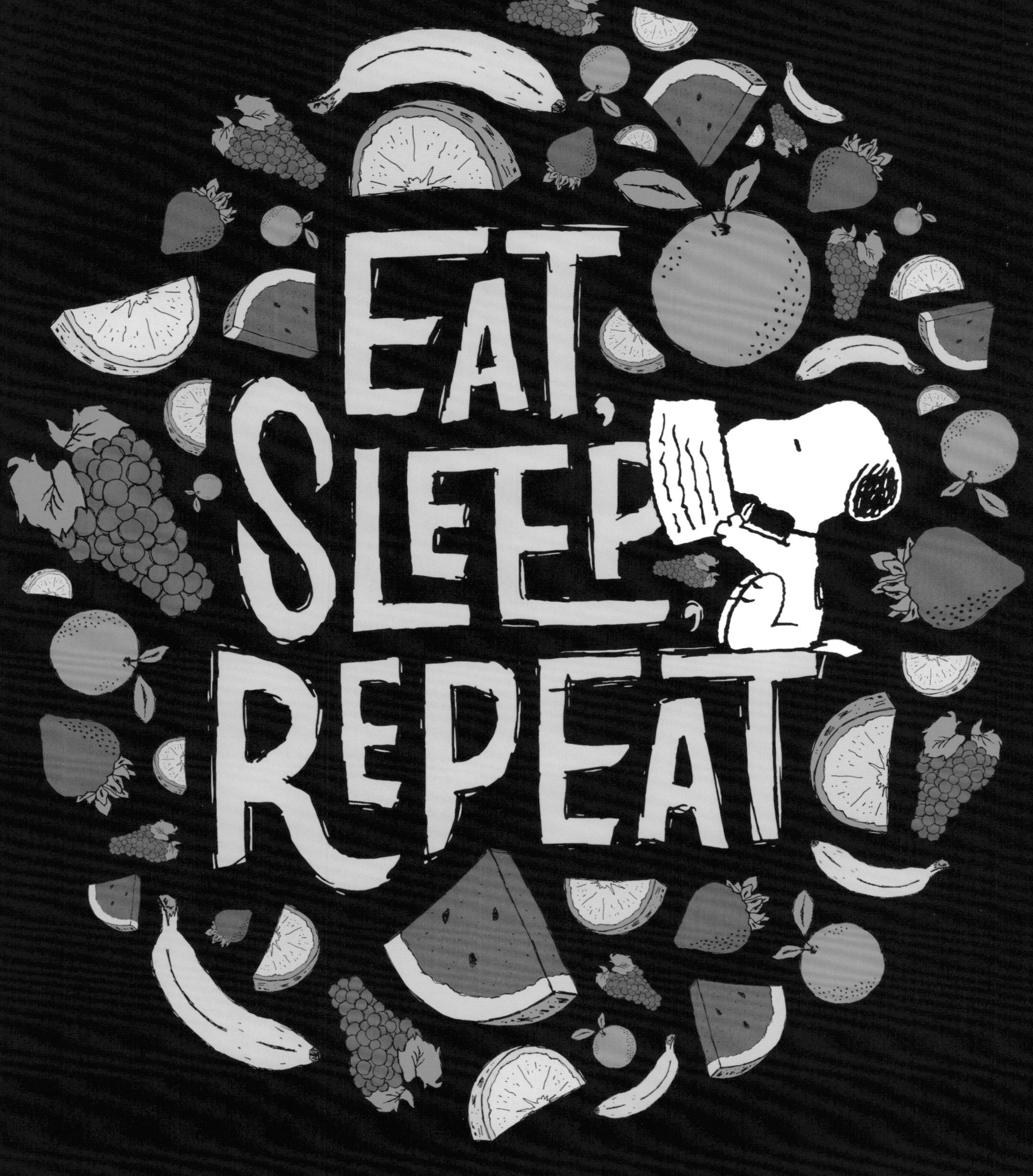
EAT, SLEEP, REPEAT

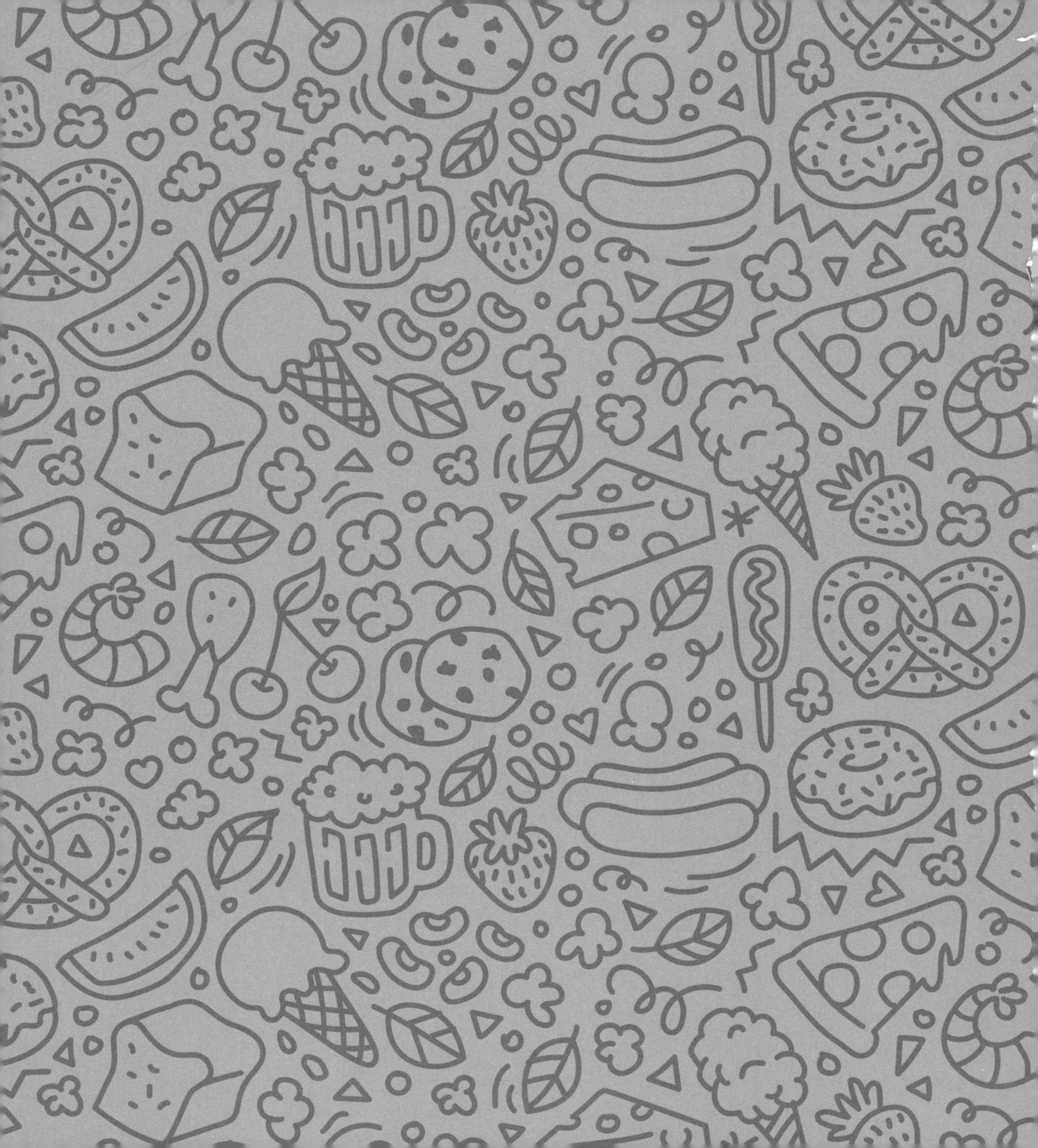